Pocket Rough Guide

AMSTERDAM

written and researched by

MARTIN DUNFORD, PHIL LEE
and KAROLINE THOMAS

Contents

INTRODUCTION TO
Amsterdam

There's nowhere quite like Amsterdam. You could be sitting nursing a drink outside one of its cafés, chugging by boat along its canals, or riding its ringing trams, and you'll sense immediately that you couldn't be anywhere else in the world. What is it that makes it so unique? Well, its watery cityscape means that much of the centre is off-limits to traffic; its architecture is for the most part on a human rather than a grandiose scale; and its people are comfortable in their skin, proud of the capacity of their city to change, but also of its uncanny – and reassuring – ability to stay much the same as it has always been.

TAKE A BOAT TRIP DOWN THE CANALS

In part it's the longstanding liberal tradition of the city that has given Amsterdam its distinctive character, beginning with the obvious – the legalized prostitution and dope-smoking coffeeshops – through to more subtle qualities, encapsulated by Amsterdammers themselves in the word *gezellig*, a very Dutch concept which roughly corresponds to "warmly convivial" – something perhaps most manifest in the city's wonderfully diverse selection of bars and cafés. The city is also riding something of a resurgent wave, with dozens of great new restaurants, a vibrant arts scene and a club scene that has come of age, not to mention the radical redevelopment of its old docklands and the rediscovery of neighbourhoods like the Oud West, de Pijp and Amsterdam Noord – a process that will only be hastened when they finally complete the Noord-Zuid metro line, whose workings have scarred the city centre for years now.

The old centre of the city spreads south from the train station, and includes Amsterdam's famous Red Light District. The layout of the rest of the city centre is determined by a web of canals radiating out from here to loop right round the centre as the so-called Grachtengordel, a planned, seventeenth-century

Best places for...a cold beer in summer

It's hard to imagine a more chilled-out place than Amsterdam in summer, and a better place to just kick back and drink beer. Here are some of our favourite spots to enjoy an alfresco *vaasje* (glass of beer): > Het Molenpad p.69 > Proust p.79 > De Sluyswacht p.93 > Gent aan de Schinkel p.101

When to visit

Amsterdam has warm, mild summers and moderately cold and wet winters. The climate is certainly not severe enough to make much difference to the city's routines, which makes Amsterdam an ideal all-year destination. That said, high summer – roughly late June to August – sees the city's parks packed to the gunnels and parts of the centre almost overwhelmed by tourists. Spring and autumn are not too crowded and can be especially beautiful, with mist hanging over the canals and low sunlight beaming through the cloud cover. Even in January and February, when things can be at their gloomiest, there are compensations – wet cobbles glistening under the street lights and the canals rippled by falling raindrops. In the summer, from around June to August, mosquitoes can be bothersome.

extension to the medieval town, with its tall, elegant gabled houses reflected in black-green waters.

There are plenty of first-rate attractions, most notably the Anne Frank Huis, the Rijksmuseum, with its wonderful collection of Dutch paintings, the peerless Van Gogh Museum and the newly renovated Stedelijk gallery of modern art. But it's not all about the sights: Amsterdam is a great city just to be in, with no attractions so important that they have to interrupt lazy days of just wandering the canals and taking in the city at your own pace. Finally, don't forget that Holland is a small country and that there are plenty of compelling attractions close by, not least the small town of Haarlem, with the great Frans Hals Museum, the Zuider Zee villages to the north, and the stunning Keukenhof Gardens – all very easy to reach by public transport.

AMSTERDAM AT A GLANCE

>> EATING

The **food** in the average Dutch restaurant has improved hugely in recent years, and there are many places serving inventive takes on homegrown cuisine. The city also has a good assortment of ethnic restaurants, especially Indonesian, Chinese and Thai. There are also lots of bars – known as *eetcafés* – that serve adventurous food for a decent price in a relaxed and unpretentious setting. Note that the Dutch eat out relatively early, with most restaurants opening at 5.30pm or 6pm and closing around 10pm.

>> COFFEESHOPS

Though their future was uncertain at the time of writing (see pp.133 & 139), Amsterdam has long been known for its **coffeeshops**, which are permitted to sell small quantities of **cannabis** and ready-made joints. The majority of coffeeshops are found in the Old Centre and generally look like regular cafés. Prevented from advertising (you need to look at a menu to see what's on offer) they usually sell a wide range of Dutch weed, grown under artificial lights as well as compressed resin such as *Pollem*. Most of it is extremely potent and to be handled with care – ask before you buy to avoid any unpleasant surprises. Coffeeshops usually open at 10am or 11am and close around midnight.

>> SHOPPING

The **Nieuwendijk/Kalverstraat** strip in the Old Centre is home to high-street fashion and mainstream department stores, while nearby **Koningsplein** and **Leidsestraat** offer designer clothes and shoe stores. You'll find more offbeat clothes shops in the Jordaan and in the small radial streets that connect the main canals – an area known as the Nine Streets. The cream of Amsterdam's antique trade is in the Spiegelkwartier, centred on **Nieuwe Spiegelstraat**. As regards **opening hours**, many shops take Monday morning off; Thursday is late-opening night, with most places staying open until 9pm.

>> DRINKING & NIGHTLIFE

Amsterdam's selection of bars range from traditional **brown cafés** – cosy places so called because of the dingy colour of their walls, stained by years of tobacco smoke – to slick **designer bars**. Most places stay open until around midnight or 1am during the week, and until 2am at weekends. Look out for the few **tasting houses** or *proeflokalen* that are left, originally the sampling rooms of small private distillers, now tiny, stand-up places specializing in *jenever* (gin); they tend to close around 8pm. The **clubbing** scene is intense, and there are lots of bars with DJs, as well as a decent array of live music options, particularly for jazz.

OUR RECOMMENDATIONS ON WHERE TO EAT, DRINK AND SHOP ARE LISTED AT THE END OF EACH PLACES CHAPTER.

Day One in Amsterdam

1 Dam Square > p.36. The heart of the city, and what better place to start?

2 Koninklijk Paleis > p.37. The confidence and pride of the Golden Age – in a building.

3 Nieuwe Kerk > p.38. No longer used as a church, but still one of the city's most impressive Gothic buildings.

4 Nine Streets > p.58. These streets connecting the main canals are the epitome of what makes Amsterdam special – full of intriguing one-off shops and cafés.

Lunch at Greenwoods > p.66. Stop off for a club sandwich by the canal at this pocket-sized gem.

5 The Grachtengordel > p.52–71. After shopping, just get lost in the web of stately seventeenth-century canals that make Amsterdam so unique.

6 Westerkerk > p.57. Rembrandt's burial place, and the city's grandest Renaissance-era landmark.

7 Anne Frank Huis > p.56. The city's most renowned – and moving – sight, bar none.

8 The Jordaan > p.72. One of the city's most wanderable and picturesque districts, full of independent stores, bars and restaurants.

Dinner at Toscanini > p.78. There's no better place to wind up of an evening than at this big, lively and very authentic Italian in the Jordaan.

Day Two in Amsterdam

1 Rijksmuseum > p.95. When it finally reopens this should be one of the finest museums in Europe; for the moment it still gives a decent glimpse of the art of the city's Golden Age.

2 Van Gogh Museum > p.97. The greatest collection of the prolific nineteenth-century artist's work by far, and with good temporary exhibits too.

Lunch at Café Loetje > p.101. Lunch on the best steaks and burgers in town, on a lovely outside terrace.

3 Begijnhof > p.44. Tucked away just off the city's main shopping street, this is an alluring unusual oasis of peace in the heart of the city.

4 Amsterdam Museum > p.45. The history of the city, well told with lots of fascinating original artefacts and clever audio-visual touches, all housed in a former orphanage.

5 Red Light District > p.39. It's hard to come to Amsterdam and not have a wander around its most notorious neighbourhood.

6 Oude Kerk > p.38. Despite being right at the centre of the Red Light District, this is the city's most interesting and historic church.

7 Amstelkring > p.40. Better-known now, but this clandestine Catholic church is still something of a hidden gem.

Dinner at Van Kerkwijk > p.50. Great little bar/restaurant in the Old Centre. There's no menu – instead the friendly staff memorize the dishes of the day.

Jewish Amsterdam

Amsterdam's Jewish Quarter is a shadow of its former self, but there are many reminders of how integral to the life of the city its Jewish population once was. Touring these sights makes for a cohesive and moving day out, especially if you wind up at the most famous Jewish sight of them all, the Anne Frank Huis.

1 Jodenbreestraat > p.82.
The heart of Amsterdam's mainly Sephardic Jewish community in seventeenth-century Amsterdam.

2 Waterlooplein > p.83. Home of the first Jewish settlement in Amsterdam, now the venue of the best flea market.

3 Joods Historisch Museum > p.85. Four converted synagogues house permanent and temporary exhibits on Jewish life in the city.

4 Esnoga > p.84. The city's Portuguese Synagogue was once one of the largest in the world.

5 Hollandse Schouwburg > p.87. The remains of a theatre that was the main assembly point for Jews being deported in World War II.

6 Verzetsmuseum > p.88. Excellent museum dedicated to the wartime resistance to the Nazis.

Lunch at Greetje > p.92. Try out some Dutch cuisine at the snug *Greetje*.

7 Gassan Diamonds > p.81. The only remnant of the main industry of the Jewish Quarter before the war.

8 Anne Frank Huis > p.56. Not in the Jewish Quarter proper, but still the city's principal – and only essential – Jewish sight.

Dinner at De Reiger > p.78, Enjoy a casual dinner at one of the Jordaan's best brown cafés.

Free Amsterdam

You can have a great day out in Amsterdam, see loads, and not spend a cent apart from a few euros on lunch and dinner. Here's how.

1 **Schuttersgalerij** > p.45. This gallery, with its portraits of civic guards, is the only free bit of the Amsterdam Museum.

2 **Begijnhof** > p.44. One of the city centre's most beguiling sights, and totally free.

3 **Bloemenmarkt** > p.63. There's no charge to wander past the stalls of the city's wonderful flower market.

(11) **Lunch: Cone of chips from Vlaminckx** > p.48. A cone of *frites* from this famed takeaway will only set you back a couple of euros.

4 **Albert Cuypmarkt** > p.103. Just wandering the length of the city's best market is a fine way to pass the time.

5 **Lunchtime concerts at the Concertgebouw/Muziektheater** > p.98/p.82. There are regular free lunchtime concerts at these two impressive arts venues.

6 **Vondelpark** > p.98. The city centre's main park is one its best attractions, and there's no charge for its weekend summer concerts either.

7 **Zeeburg** > p.90 Take a walk or, better, cycle around Amsterdam's up-and-coming districts to the east of Centraal Station.

8 **Ferries across the IJ** > Take one of the free ferries from behind Centraal Station to Amsterdam Noord and discover leafy suburbs, perfect for aimless wandering.

(11) **Dinner at Bird** > p.49 Fill up on Tom Yum soup, sweet spare ribs and well-priced vegetarian dishes at this busy little Thai canteen.

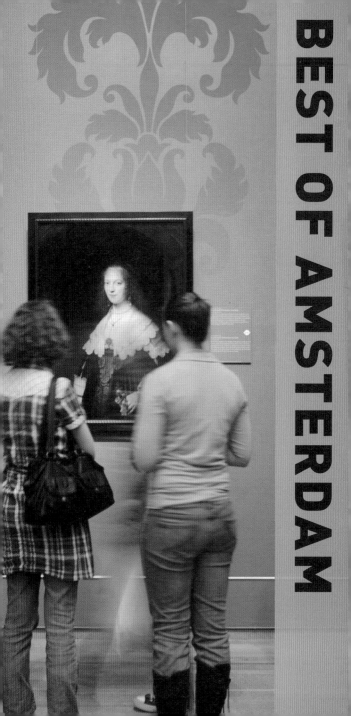

Big sights

1 **Van Gogh Museum** With the world's most comprehensive collection of the artist's work, this museum is simply unmissable. **> p.97**

2 Red Light District Although recently spruced up, Amsterdam's red light district is still the real thing – and a big attraction in its own right. **> p.39**

3 The Rijksmuseum Due to reopen in 2013, the Rijksmuseum will once again take its place as one of the world's great museums. **> p.98**

4 Anne Frank Huis The secret annexe where the diarist hid with her family during the Nazi occupation is Amsterdam's most moving tourist attraction. **> p.56**

5 Koninklijk Paleis The supreme architectural example of the Dutch empire at the height of its powers. **> p.37**

Museums and galleries

1 Rijksmuseum The Rijksmuseum's unrivalled collection of seventeenth-century Dutch art should be fully unveiled in 2013. **> p.95**

2 Amstelkring Once a clandestine church for the city's Catholics, the seventeenth-century house chapel is a very distinctive sight. > **p.40**

4 Stedelijk Musem Newly expanded and renovated, Amsterdam's world-class modern art museum is simply unmissable. > **p.98**

3 Van Gogh Museum The greatest collection of Van Gogh's work, along with the paintings and Japanese prints that influenced him. > **p.97**

5 Amsterdam Museum An excellent museum devoted to the life and times of the city. > **p.45**

Waterfront

1 Queen's Day The one day of the year when anarchy reigns on the city's canals. Don't miss it. **> p.136**

2 Brouwersgracht The dolled-up former warehouses here make this one of the city's most picturesque canals. > **p.52**

3 Blijburg The ultimate urban beach in summer. > **p.91**

4 De Sluyswacht This bar in a rickety old lock-keeper's house is a wonderful place to have a drink. > **p.93**

5 Zeeburg Cutting-edge new architecture and design, and lots of waterside bars and restaurants to enjoy it from. > **p.90**

Coffeeshops

1 **Abraxas** Lots of levels to negotiate via spiral staircases make this cosy place challenging after a spliff or two. > **p.47**

2 Kadinsky Always busy, and serves great cookies and hot chocolate too. > **p.47**

3 Hill Street Blues
Favoured for its comfy sofas and chilled-out vibe, with two locations right in the heart of the Red Light District. > **p.47**

4 Barney's Once known for its great breakfast, now for the quality of its dope. > **p.76**

5 Dampkring Loud and friendly city-centre hangout with excellent hash and weed at good prices. > **p.47**

Restaurants

1 Moeders Proper Dutch food at moderate prices. **> p.78**

2 Greetje Great service, fantastic modern Dutch food. > **p.92**

4 Toscanini One of the city centre's best Italian restaurants – big, bustling and authentic. > **p.78**

3 Blauw aan de Wal A wonderful, peaceful culinary haven right in the heart of the Red Light District. > **p.49**

5 De Belhamel Great-value Dutch cooking on picturesque Brouwersgracht. > **p.66**

Bars

1 Wynand Fockink Perhaps the city's best example of an old-fashioned *proeflokaal* or "tasting-house". **> p.51**

2 In 't Aepjen Right on Zeedijk, this is one of the city's top brown cafés. > **p.51**

4 Hoppe There's nowhere quite like *Hoppe*, or the crowd that winds up here, especially after everywhere else has closed. > **p.51**

3 Café 't Arendsnest This friendly canal house bar is the best place to try Dutch beers from all over the country. > **p.68**

5 't Smalle One of the city's oldest and cosiest cafés, with a lovely waterside terrace. > **p.79**

Nightlife and Culture

1 Bimhuis Amsterdam's premier jazz venue, next door to the Muziekgebouw.
> **p.93**

2 Jimmy Woo East meets West at this loungey club, where the stylish come out to play and the dancefloor heaves to the sound of disco and club classics. **> p.70**

4 Melkweg This Sixties favourite remains the city's prime venue for inventive and original performing arts. **> p.71**

3 Bitterzoet Spacious but snug bar and theatre that hosts club nights and early evening live music and performance art. **> p.51**

5 Paradiso One of the city's oldest venue for live music, and still the best. **> p.71**

Shopping

1 Puccini The unusually good chocolates are made on the premises at their two city centre locations. > **p.47 & 65**

2 The Nine Streets Hosts some of the city's quirkiest one-off stores – well worth a wander. > **p.58**

3 Condomerie Het Gulden Vlies The ultimate specialist shop, and a useful one too, with a mind-boggling array of prophylactics. > **p.46**

5 Droog Not quite like any other shop you may have been to... > **p.46**

4 Albert Cuypmarkt Busy general market that is still to some extent the authentic heart of working-class Amsterdam. > **p.103**

The Old Centre

Amsterdam's most vivacious district, the Old Centre is a tangle of antique streets and narrow canals, confined in the north by the River IJ and to the west and south by the Singel. Given the dominance of Centraal Station on most transport routes, this is where you'll almost certainly arrive. From here a stroll across the bridge will take you onto the Damrak, which divided the Oude Zijde (Old Side) of the medieval city to the east from the smaller Nieuwe Zijde (New Side) to the west. It also leads to the heart of the Old Centre, Dam Square, the site of the city's most imperious building, the Royal Palace (Koninklijk Paleis). Nowadays much of the Oude Zijde is taken up by the city's notorious Red Light District – but the area is about more than just sleaze: its main canals and the houses that line them are among Amsterdam's most handsome. And the Old Centre as a whole hosts some of the city's best bars and restaurants alongside what can only be described as tourist tat.

CENTRAAL STATION

MAP PP.34–35, POCKET MAP C10–C11

With its high gables and cheerful brickwork, **Centraal Station** is an imposing prelude to the city. Built in the 1880s, it aroused much controversy because it effectively separated the centre from the River IJ, source of the city's wealth, for the first time in Amsterdam's long history. Inside, the cavernous main booking hall and grand arches have a suitable sense of occasion, and from here the whole of Amsterdam lies before you. However, for the moment, **Stationsplein** just outside is a pretty unprepossessing introduction to the city: a messy open space, edged by ovals of water and cut through by trams. It's currently dominated by the building works of the city's new north-south transport link, which is taking a lot longer to complete than expected. Once the metro is finished, expect a much spruced-up open space (see box opposite).

TRAMS AT CENTRAAL STATION

ST NICOLAASKERK

Prins Hendrikkade 73 ☎ 020/624 8749. Mon & Sat noon–3pm, Tues–Fri 11am–4pm. Free. MAP PP.34–35, POCKET MAP O11

Dating back to the 1880s, the city's foremost Catholic church, with its whopping twin towers and spacious interior is dedicated to the patron saint of sailors – and of Amsterdam. Above the altar is the crown of the Habsburg Emperor Maximilian, very much a symbol of the city.

DAMRAK

MAP PP.34–35, POCKET MAP C11

Running from Centraal Station to Dam Square, **Damrak** was a canal and the city's main nautical artery until 1672, when it was filled in – much to the relief of the locals, who were tired of the stink. With the docks moved elsewhere, Damrak became a busy commercial drag, as it remains today: an unenticing avenue lined with tacky restaurants, bars and bureaux de change.

Got the builders in?

Centraal Station and the inner harbour have frankly looked a bit of a mess for as long as most people can remember, due to a long-running project to redevelop the station and the surrounding area at the same time as building a new metro line to link the city centre with the south of the city and the resurgent north across the River IJ. Metro stations are to be built at Centraal Station, Rokin and the Vijzelgracht, and for the best part of six years now the area around Stationsplein has been a massive construction site – and the chaos looks set to continue for some time, at least until the completion of the project in 2015. There has been huge controversy over the plan: some question whether it's even possible to construct a tunnel under a city centre that is mainly built on wooden stilts, and work was halted for a while a couple of years back when a number of buildings began to collapse. But the authorities are determined to press on, and claim they will not only deliver better connections between the city centre and outlying districts, but also a pedestrian-friendly Stationsplein and inner harbour. Whatever the result, it will seem like an improvement after the last few years.

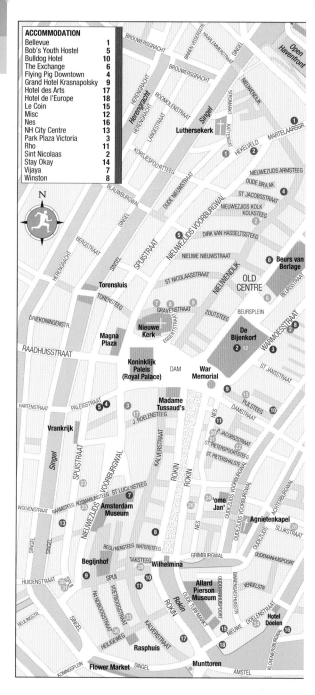

ACCOMMODATION

Bellevue	1
Bob's Youth Hostel	5
Bulldog Hotel	10
The Exchange	6
Flying Pig Downtown	4
Grand Hotel Krasnapolsky	9
Hotel des Arts	17
Hotel de l'Europe	18
Le Coin	15
Misc	12
Nes	16
NH City Centre	13
Park Plaza Victoria	3
Rho	11
Sint Nicolaas	2
Stay Okay	14
Vijaya	7
Winston	8

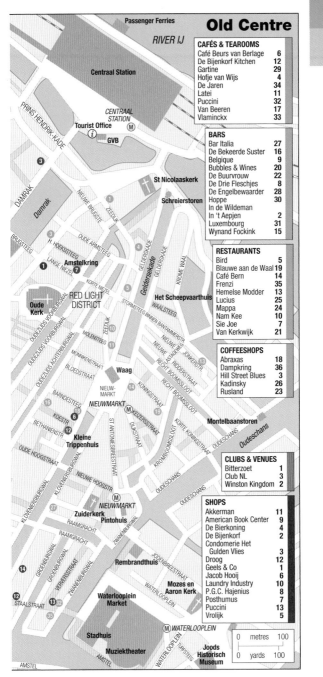

Old Centre

CAFÉS & TEAROOMS

Café Beurs van Berlage	6
De Bijenkorf Kitchen	12
Gartine	29
Hofje van Wijs	4
De Jaren	34
Latei	11
Puccini	32
Van Beeren	17
Vlaminckx	33

BARS

Bar Italia	27
De Bekeerde Suster	16
Belgique	9
Bubbles & Wines	20
De Buurvrouw	22
De Drie Fleschjes	8
De Engelbewaarder	28
Hoppe	30
In de Wildeman	
In 't Aepjen	2
Luxembourg	31
Wynand Fockink	15

RESTAURANTS

Bird	5
Blauwe aan de Waal	19
Café Bern	14
Frenzi	35
Hemelse Modder	13
Lucius	25
Mappa	24
Nam Kee	10
Sie Joe	7
Van Kerkwijk	21

COFFEESHOPS

Abraxas	18
Dampkring	36
Hill Street Blues	3
Kadinsky	26
Rusland	23

CLUBS & VENUES

Bitterzoet	1
Club NL	3
Winston Kingdom	2

SHOPS

Akkerman	11
American Book Center	9
De Bierkoning	4
De Bijenkorf	2
Condomerie Het Gulden Vlies	3
Droog	12
Geels & Co	1
Jacob Hooij	6
Laundry Industry	10
P.G.C. Hajenius	8
Posthumus	7
Puccini	13
Vrolijk	5

Passenger Ferries

RIVER IJ

Centraal Station

CENTRAAL STATION

Tourist Office

GVB

PRINS HENDRIK-KADE

St Nicolaaskerk

Schreierstoren

NIEUWE BRUGSTE

ZEEDIJK

DAMRAK

Damrak

BRUGSTEEG

H. HOEKSSTEEG

LANGE NIEZEL

OUDE ARMSTEEG

KORTE NIEZEL

Amstelkring

Oude Kerk

RED LIGHT DISTRICT

GELDERSKADE

GELDERSKADE

KROME WAAL

Het Scheepvaarthuis

WAALSTEEG

STORMSTEEG BINNEN BANTAMMERSTR

OUDEZIJDS VOORBURGWAL

OUDEZIJDS VOORBURGWAL

OUDEZIJDS ACHTERBURGWAL

MOLENSTEEG

ZEEDIJK

MONNIKENSTRAAT

BLOEDSTRAAT

NIEUWE JONKERSTR

NIEUWE JONKERSTR

RIDDERSTRAAT

RECHT BOOMSSTR

RECHT BOOMSSLOOT

Waag

NIEUW-MARKT

KONINGSTRAAT

BARNDESTEEG

KOESTR

BETHANIENSTR

Kleine Trippenhuis

NIEUWMARKT

KEIZERSSTRAAT

ST ANTONIESBREESTRAAT

DIJKSTRAAT

KORTE KONINGSTRAAT

Montelbaanstoren

Oudeschans

KROMBOOMSSLOOT

OUDE HOOGSTRAAT

NIEUWE HOOGSTR

OUDESCHANS

OUDESCHANS

KLOVENIERSBURGWAL

Zuiderkerk

Pintohuis

NIEUWMARKT

RAAMGRACHT

RAAMGRACHT

Rembrandthuis

ZWANENBURGWAL

JODENBREESTRAAT

Mozes en Aaron Kerk

GROENBURGWAL

GROCABURGWAL

VERWERSSTRAAT

ZWANENBURGWAL

Waterlooplein Market

WATERLOOPLEIN

STAALSTRAAT

Stadhuis

Muziektheater

AMSTEL

WATERLOOPLEIN

WATERLOOPLEIN

TURFSTEEG

Joods Historisch Museum

0	metres	100
0	yards	100

CYCLING IN DAM SQUARE

THE BEURS VAN BERLAGE

Damrak 243 ☎ 020/531 3355, ⓦ www
.beursvanberlage.nl. MAP PP.34-35, POCKET MAP
B11-C11

The imposing bulk of the
Beurs – the old Stock
Exchange – is a seminal work
designed at the turn of the
twentieth century by the
leading light of the Dutch
modern movement, **Hendrik
Petrus Berlage**. Berlage
re-routed Dutch architecture
with this building, forsaking
the classicism that had
dominated the nineteenth
century for a modern style with
cleaner lines. The Beurs has
long since lost its commercial
function and today it's used for
exhibitions, concerts and
conferences, which means that
sometimes you can go in,
sometimes you can't. Inside, the
main hall is distinguished by
the graceful lines of its exposed
ironwork and its
shallow-arched arcades as well
as the fanciful frieze celebrating
the stockbroker's trade. If it's
closed, stop by the café that
fronts onto Beursplein around
the corner (see p.48) for a
coffee and admire the tiled
scenes of the past, present and
the future by Jan Toorop.

DAM SQUARE

MAP PP.34-35, POCKET MAP B12

It was **Dam Square** that gave
Amsterdam its name: in the
thirteenth century the River
Amstel was dammed here, and
the fishing village that grew
around it became known as
"Amstelredam". Boats could
sail into the square down the
Damrak and unload right in
the middle of the settlement,
which soon prospered by
trading herrings for Baltic
grain. Today it's an open and
airy but somehow rather
desultory square, despite the
presence of the main
municipal war memorial, a
prominent stone tusk adorned
by bleak, suffering figures and
decorated with the coats of
arms of each of the
Netherlands' provinces (plus
the ex-colony of Indonesia).

MADAME TUSSAUDS

Dam Square 243 ☎ 020/522 1010 ⓦ www
.madametussauds.com/amsterdam. Daily
10am-5.30pm. €21, children 5-15 €16. MAP
PP.34-35, POCKET MAP B12

The Amsterdam branch of the
Madame Tussauds empire
provides waxwork Dutch royals
and footballers alongside the
usual international celebs.

THE KONINKLIJK PALEIS

Dam Square ☎ 020/620 4060 ⓦ www
.paleisamsterdam.nl. June–Aug daily
11am–5pm, otherwise daily noon–5pm, but
closed on Royal occasions as detailed on the
website. €7.50.. MAP PP.34–35, POCKET MAP B12

Dominating Dam Square is the
Koninklijk Paleis (Royal
Palace) though the title is
deceptive, given that this vast
structure started out as the city's
town hall and only had its first
royal occupant when Louis
Bonaparte, brother of
Napoleon, moved in during the
French occupation.

At the time of the building's
construction in the
mid-seventeenth century,
Amsterdam was at the height of
its powers, and the city council
craved a residence that was a
suitable declaration of its wealth
and independence. The **exterior**
is full of maritime symbolism,
hinting at the trade routes that
made the city rich. The **interior**
proclaims the pride and
confidence of Amsterdam's
Golden Age, principally in the
lavish **Citizen's Hall** where the
enthroned figure of Amsterdam
looks down on the earth and
the heavens, laid out before her
in three circular, inlaid marble
maps. Other allegorical **figures**
ram home the municipal point:
flanking "Amsterdam" to the
left and right are Wisdom and
Strength, and the relief to the
right shows Mercury
attempting to lull Argos to
sleep – stressing the need to be
vigilant. All this is part of a
witty symbolism that pervades
the Hall and the surrounding
galleries: in the top-left gallery,
cocks fight above the entrance
to the Commissioner of Petty
Affairs and above the door of
the Bankruptcy Chamber, in
the gallery to the right of the
main hall, a medallion shows
the Fall of Icarus below marble
carvings depicting hungry rats
nibbling at unpaid bills.

The decorative whimsy fizzles
out in the intimidating and
cramped **High Court of Justice**
at the front of the building.
Here, magistrates sat on marble
benches overseen by
heavyweight representations of
Righteousness, Wisdom and
Mercy as they passed
judgement on the hapless
criminals in front of them;
even worse, the baying crowd
on Dam Square could view the
proceedings through the barred
windows. If a death sentence
was passed, the condemned
were whisked up to the wooden
scaffold attached to the front of
the building and promptly
dispatched.

THE KONINKLIJK PALEIS

OUDE KERK

MAGNA PLAZA

Nieuwezijds Voorburgwal 182 ☎ 020/421 1717, ⓦ www.magnaplaza.nl. Mon 11am–7pm, Tues–Sat 10am–7pm, Thurs until 9pm, Sun noon–7pm. MAP PP.34–35, POCKET MAP A12

Behind the Royal Palace, you can't miss the old neo-Gothic post office of 1899, now converted into the **Magna Plaza** shopping mall, housing numerous clothes chains.

OUDE KERK

Oudekerksplein ☎ 020/625 8284, ⓦ www .oudekerk.nl. Church: Mon–Sat 11am–5pm, Sun 1–5pm. €5. Tower: April–Sept 1–5pm; €7. MAP PP.34–35, POCKET MAP C12

Tucked away in the Red Light District, the **Oude Kerk** is the city's most appealing church. There's been a church on this site since the middle of the thirteenth century, but most of the present building dates from a century later, funded by the pilgrims who came here in their hundreds following a widely publicized miracle. The story goes that in 1345 a dying man regurgitated the Host he had received here at Communion and when it was thrown on the fire afterwards, it did not burn. The unburnable Host was placed in a chest and eventually installed here, and although it disappeared during the Reformation, thousands of the faithful still come to take part in the annual commemorative **Stille Omgang** in mid-March, a silent nocturnal procession terminating at the Oude Kerk. Inside the church you can see the unadorned memorial tablet of Rembrandt's first wife, Saskia van Uylenburg, beneath the smaller of the organs, and three beautifully coloured stained-glass windows beside the ambulatory dating from the 1550s. It's possible to climb the church tower in summer.

THE NIEUWE KERK

Dam Square ☎ 020/626 8168, ⓦ www .nieuwekerk.nl. Daily 10am–5pm, Thurs until 10pm. €15. MAP PP.34–35, POCKET MAP B12

Vying for importance with the Royal Palace is the adjacent **Nieuwe Kerk**, which despite its name – "new church" – is an early fifteenth-century structure built in a late flourish of the Gothic style, with a forest of pinnacles and high, slender gables. Nowadays it's de-sanctified and used for temporary exhibitions. Opening times vary according to what's on, and occasionally it's closed altogether when exhibitions are being changed. But it is worth going in if you can: its hangar-like interior holds a scattering of decorative highlights, such as the seventeenth-century tomb of Dutch naval hero Admiral Michiel de Ruyter, complete with trumpeting angels, conch-blowing Neptunes and cherubs all in a tizzy.

The Red Light District

The area to the east of Damrak, between Warmoesstraat, Nieuwmarkt and Damstraat, is the **Red Light District**, known locally as "De Walletjes" (Small Walls) on account of the series of low brick walls that contains its canals. The district stretches across the two narrow canals that once marked the eastern limits of medieval Amsterdam, **Oudezijds Voorburgwal** and **Oudezijds Achterburgwal**. The area is pretty seedy, although the legalized prostitution here has long been one of the city's most distinctive draws. It wasn't always so: the handsome facades of Oudezijds Voorburgwal in particular recall ritzier days when this was one of the wealthiest parts of the city, richly earning its nickname the "Velvet Canal".

Oudezijds Voorburgwal and Oudezijds Achterburgwal, with their narrow connecting passages, are thronged with "**window brothels**", and at busy times the crass, on-street haggling over the price of sex is drowned out by a surprisingly festive atmosphere – entire families grinning more or less amiably at the women in the windows or discussing the specifications of the sex toys in the shops. Nonetheless, there is a nasty undertow to the district, oddly enough sharper during the daytime, when the pimps hang out in shifty gangs and drug addicts wait anxiously, assessing the chances of scoring their next hit. Don't even think about taking a picture of one of the windows, unless you're prepared for some major grief from the camera-shy prostitutes and their minders.

What's more, the whole **future** of the Red Light district is under threat. The trafficking of women to fill the window brothels – and the illegal clandestine brothels – has become something of a municipal scandal and there have been political manoeuvres to have the whole area closed down or moved way out of the city. At the moment, there's a deadlock in the situation, but it's hard to say quite how the issue will be resolved.

THE AMSTELKRING

Oudezijds Voorburgwal 40 ☎ 020/624 6604,
ⓦ www.museumamstelkring.nl. Mon–Sat
10am–5pm, Sun 1–5pm. €8. MAP PP.34–35,
POCKET MAP C11

A few metres north of the Oude Kerk (see p.38) is the lovely **Amstelkring**, a former Catholic church, now one of Amsterdam's most enjoyable museums. The Amstelkring – "Amstel Circle" – is named after the group of nineteenth-century historians who saved the building from demolition, but its proper name is Ons Lieve Heer Op Solder ("Our Dear Lord in the Attic"). The church dates from the early seventeenth century when the city's Catholics were only allowed to practise their faith in private – as here in this clandestine church, which occupies the loft of a wealthy merchant's house. The church's narrow nave has been skilfully shoehorned into the available space and, flanked by elegant balconies, there's just enough room for an ornately carved

organ at one end and a mock-marble high altar, decorated with Jacob de Wit's mawkish *Baptism of Christ*, at the other. The rest of the house is similarly untouched, its original furnishings reminiscent of interiors by Vermeer or De Hooch.

HASH MARIHUANA & HEMP MUSEUM

Oudezijds Achterburgwal 148 ☎ 020/623 5961,
ⓦ www.hashmuseum.com. Daily 10am–11pm.
€9. MAP PP.34–35, POCKET MAP C12

The **Hash Marihuana & Hemp Museum** claims to hold the "world's largest collection of cannabis-related artefacts" and features displays on different kinds of dope and the huge number of ways to imbibe and otherwise use it. Among the 6,000 items on show are old tins of prescription cannabis, a hemp electric guitar and running shoes, plus pamphlets explaining the medicinal properties of weed. There's also a shop selling pipes, books, videos and plenty of souvenirs.

NIEUWMARKT

MAP PP.34–35, POCKET MAP C12

On the far side of the Red Light District is the Nieuwmarkt, a wide open cobbled square that was long one of the city's most important markets. Its main focus is the multi-turreted **Waag**, a delightful building dating from the 1480s, when it served as one of the city's fortified gates, the Sint Antoniespoort, before being turned into a municipal weighing-house (*waag*), with the rooms upstairs taken over by the surgeons' guild. It was here that the surgeons held lectures on anatomy and public dissections, the inspiration for Rembrandt's famous *Anatomy Lesson of Dr Tulp*. It has now

THE AMSTELKRING

been converted into a café-bar and restaurant, *In de Waag*.

THE SCHREIERSTOREN

Geldersekade. MAP PP.34–35, POCKET MAP D11–D12

A few minutes' walk north from Nieuwmarkt, the squat **Schreierstoren** (Weepers' Tower) is a rare surviving chunk of the city's medieval wall. Originally, the tower overlooked the River IJ and it was here (legend has it) that women gathered to watch their menfolk sail away – hence its name. A badly weathered stone plaque inserted in the wall is a reminder of all those sad goodbyes, and another much more recent plaque recalls the departure of Henry Hudson from here in 1609, when he stumbled across an island the locals called Manhattan.

HET SCHEEPVAARTHUIS

Prins Hendrikkade 108. MAP PP.34–35, POCKET MAP D12

Now occupied by the five-star *Amrath* hotel, this is one of the city's most flamboyant Expressionist buildings, covered with a welter of marine connections – the entrance is shaped like the prow of a ship, and surmounted by statues of Poseidon and his wife, and representations of the four points of the compass.

KLOVENIERSBURGWAL

MAP PP.34–35, POCKET MAP C12–C13

Nieuwmarkt lies at the northern end of Kloveniersburgwal, a long, dead-straight waterway framed by old, dignified facades. One house of special note is the **Trippenhuis**, at no. 29, a huge overblown mansion built for the Trip family in 1662. One of the richest families in Amsterdam, the Trips were one of a clique of families (Six, Trip, Hooft and Pauw) who shared power during the city's Golden Age.

Almost directly opposite, on the west bank of the canal, the **Kleine Trippenhuis** at no. 26 is, by contrast, one of the narrowest houses in Amsterdam, complete with a warmly carved facade with a balustrade featuring centaurs and sphinxes. Legend asserts that Mr Trip's coachman was so taken aback by the size of the new family mansion that he exclaimed he would be happy with a home no wider than the Trips' front door – which is exactly what he got.

ST ANTONIESBREESTRAAT

MAP PP.34–35, POCKET MAP C12–C13

Stretching south from the wide open spaces of the Nieuwmarkt, **St Antoniesbreestraat** once linked the city centre with the Jewish quarter, but its huddle of shops and houses was mostly demolished in the 1980s to make way for a main road. The plan was subsequently abandoned, but the modern buildings that now line most of the street hardly fire the soul, even if the modern symmetries – and cubist, coloured panels – of the apartment blocks that spill along part of the street are visually arresting.

THE PINTOHUIS

St Antoniesbreestraat 69. ☎ 020/624 3184, ⓦwww.oba.nl. Mon 2–8pm, Wed & Fri 10am–5.30pm, Sat 11am–4pm. Free. MAP PP.34–35, POCKET MAP D13

One of the few survivors of all the development along St Antoinebreestraat is the **Pintohuis**, which is now a public library. Easily spotted by its off-white Italianate facade, the mansion is named after

Isaac de Pinto, a Jew who fled Portugal to escape the Inquisition and subsequently became a founder of the East India Company. Pinto bought the property in 1651 and promptly had it remodelled in grand style, the facade interrupted by six lofty pilasters, which lead the eye up to the blind balustrade. The mansion was the talk of the town, even more so when Pinto had the interior painted in a similar style to the front – pop in to look at the birds and cherubs of the original painted ceiling.

THE ZUIDERKERK

Zuiderkerkhof ☎ 020/689 2565, ⓦwww. uiderkerkamsterdam.nl. Church: Mon–Fri 9am–4pm, Sat noon–4pm. Free. Tower: April– Sept Mon–Sat 1–5pm.€7. MAP PP.34–35, POCKET MAP C13

The **Zuiderkerk** dates from 1611 and was designed by the prolific architect and sculptor Hendrick de Keyser, whose distinctive – and very popular – style extrapolated elements of traditional Flemish design, with fanciful detail added wherever possible. The soaring tower is typical of his work and comes complete with balconies and balustrades, arches and columns. Now deconsecrated, the church has been turned into a municipal information centre with displays on housing and the environment, plus temporary exhibitions revealing the city council's future plans. The tower, which has a separate entrance, can be climbed during the summer.

OUDEMANHUISPOORT

MAP PP.34–35, POCKET MAP B14

At the south end of Kloveniersburgwal, on the right, the **Oudemanhuispoort** is a covered passageway whose sides are lined with

PINTOHUIS

ZUIDERKERK

secondhand bookstalls (Mon–Sat 10am–4pm); it was formerly part of an almshouse complex for elderly men – hence the unusual name. The buildings on either side are part of the University of Amsterdam, which dominates this part of town. You can either wander through its peaceful precincts or, just beyond, cross the south end of **Kloveniersburgwal** to one of the prettiest corners of the city – a small pocket of old canal houses that extends east to **Groenburgwal**, a delightful, dead-end canal.

ROKIN AND KALVERSTRAAT

MAP PP.34–35, POCKET MAP B12–B14

The **Rokin** picks up where the Damrak leaves off, cutting south from Dam Square in a wide sweep that follows the former course of the River Amstel. This was the business centre of the nineteenth-century city, and although it has lost much of its prestige it is still flanked by an attractive medley of architectural styles incorporating everything from grandiose nineteenth-century

mansions to more utilitarian modern stuff. Running parallel, pedestrianized **Kalverstraat** is a busy shopping street that has been a commercial centre since medieval times, when it was used as a calf market; nowadays it's home to many of the city's chain stores and clothes shops – you could be anywhere in Europe really.

ALLARD PIERSON MUSEUM

Oude Turfmarkt 127 ☎ 020/525 2556, ⓦ www.allardpiersonmuseum.nl. Tues–Fri 10am–5pm, Sat & Sun 1–5pm. €6.50. MAP PP.34–35, POCKET MAP B13–B14

A good old-fashioned archeological museum in a solid Neoclassical building dating from the 1860s, the **Allard Pierson Museum** holds a wide-ranging but fairly small collection of finds retrieved from Egypt, Greece and Italy. The particular highlights are the museum's Greek pottery, with fine examples of both the black- and red-figured wares produced in the sixth and fifth centuries BC, and several ornate Roman sarcophagi.

HOTEL DOELEN

Nieuwe Doelenstraat 24. MAP PP.34–35, POCKET MAP C14

Just across the canal from Muntplein, the **Hotel Doelen** incorporates the Kloveniers Tower, and was once the headquarters and meeting place of the company Rembrandt depicted in his famous painting *The Night Watch*. No one knows for sure whether he painted the famous work here, but it certainly hung in the building for a time, and if you ask nicely in reception they will let you stroll up to see where it was, although there's not much to look at beyond crumbling redbrick wall and a bad photo of the painting.

HEILIGEWEG AND SPUI

MAP PP.34–35, POCKET MAP A14

Crossing Kalverstraat, **Heiligeweg**, or "Holy Way", was once part of a much longer route used by pilgrims heading into Amsterdam. Every other religious reference disappeared centuries ago, but there is one interesting edifice here, the fanciful gateway of the old **Rasphuis** (House of Correction) that now fronts a shopping mall at the foot of Voetboogstraat. The gateway is surmounted by a sculpture of a woman punishing two criminals chained at her sides above the single word "Castigatio" (punishment). Beneath is a carving by Hendrik de Keyser showing wolves and lions cringing before the whip.

Cut up Voetboogstraat and you soon reach the **Spui**, whose west end opens out into a wide, tram-clanking intersection in the middle of which is a cloying statue of a young boy, known as *'t Lieverdje* ("Little Darling" or "Loveable Scamp"), a gift to the city from a cigarette company in 1960. It was here in the mid-1960s, with the statue seen as a symbol of the addicted consumer, that the playful political mavericks, the Provos, organized some of their most successful public pranks. There's a small secondhand book market here on Friday mornings.

THE BEGIJNHOF

Spui ☎ 020/622 1918, ⦿ www .begijnhofamsterdam.nl. Daily 8am–5pm. Free. MAP PP.34–35, POCKET MAP A13

A little gateway on the north side of the Spui leads into the **Begijnhof**, where a huddle of immaculately maintained old houses looks onto a central green; if this door is locked, try the main entrance, 200m north of the Spui on Gedempte Begijnensloot. The Begijnhof was founded in the fourteenth century as a home for the *beguines* – members of a Catholic sisterhood living as nuns, but without vows and with the right of return to the secular world. The original medieval complex comprised a series of humble brick cottages, but these were mostly replaced by the larger, grander houses of today shortly after the Reformation, though the secretive, enclosed design survived.

The **Engelse Kerk** which takes up one side of the

Begijnhof is of medieval construction, but it was taken from the *beguines* and given to Amsterdam's English community during the Reformation and is of interest for the carefully worked panels on the pulpit, which were designed by a youthful Piet Mondriaan. The *beguines*, meanwhile, celebrated Mass inconspicuously in the clandestine Catholic **Begijnhof Kapel**, which they established in the house opposite their old church, and this is still used today, a homely and very devout place, full of paintings and with large balconies on either side of the main nave.

AMSTERDAM MUSEUM

Sint Luciënsteeg 27 & Kalverstraat 92
☏ 020/523 1822, ⓦ www.amsterdammuseum. nl. Daily 10am–5pm. €10; audio-tour €4.. MAP PP.34–35, POCKET MAP A13

The **Amsterdam Museum**, which occupies the rambling seventeenth-century buildings of the former municipal orphanage, surveys the city's development from its origins as an insignificant fishing village to its present incarnation as a major metropolis and trading centre. The museum is divided into three main sections with the first providing an overview by means of a series of short films branded as "**Amsterdam DNA**". Film clips run continuously giving an insight into key events that have shaped the city's history, from the Nazi occupation to the street rioting of the 1980s. There are also longer clips exploring, for example, the architectural evolution of the city and the devastating floods that hit most of the Netherlands in 1953.

Thereafter, the second (and most confusing) section has a

AMSTERDAM MUSEUM

series of thematic displays in roughly chronological order – Amsterdam in the Golden Age, maritime trade, municipal charity and so forth. Maps and plans show the city's evolution from the draining of the Amstel in 1274 to the present day and include Cornelis Anthonisz's superbly detailed *Bird's Eye View of Amsterdam*, dating from 1538. The highlight here, though, is the **paintings**, including a whole series showing the city's regents to best advantage, self-contented bourgeois giving succour to the grateful poor; here also, in the medical care section, is **Rembrandt**'s wonderful *Anatomy Lesson of Dr Jan Deijman*.

Attached to the main body of the museum is an open-air **courtyard**, where a set of wooden lockers show where the orphans would stow their kit, and a **glassed-in passageway**, which is used for temporary exhibitions of group portraits – anything from Johan Cruyff and his footballing chums to paintings of the Amsterdam militia in their seventeenth-century pomp.

Shops

AKKERMAN

Kalverstraat 149. Mon–Fri 10am–5.45pm, Thurs until 8.45pm, Sat 10am–5pm, Sun noon–5pm. MAP PP.34–35, POCKET MAP B13

The city's poshest pen shop, with an excellent selection of pens and writing accessories.

AMERICAN BOOK CENTER

Spui 12. Mon 11am–8pm, Tues–Sat 10am–8pm, Thurs until 9pm, Sun 11am–6pm. MAP PP.34–35, POCKET MAP A13

A great stock of books in English, and one of the city's best sources of English-language magazines and newspapers.

DE BIERKONING

Paleisstraat 125. Mon 1–7pm, Tues–Fri 11am–7pm, Sat noon–6pm, Sun 1–6pm. MAP PP.34–35, POCKET MAP A12

The "Beer King" is aptly named: 950 different beers, with the appropriate glasses to drink them from – just in case you thought beer-drinking could be taken lightly.

DE BIJENKORF

Dam 1. Sun & Mon 11am–7pm, Tues & Wed 10am–7pm, Thurs & Fri 10am–9pm, Sat 9.30am–7pm. MAP PP.34–35, POCKET MAP B12

The city's top department store, good for clothes, accessories and kids' stuff.

CONDOMERIE HET GULDEN VLIES

Warmoesstraat 141. Mon–Sat 11am–6pm. MAP PP.34–35, POCKET MAP B12

Perhaps the world's most famous condom shop, selling condoms of every shape, size and flavour imaginable.

DROOG

Staalstraat 7b. Tues–Sat 11am–6pm, Sun noon–5pm. MAP PP.34–35, POCKET MAP C14

The Amsterdam HQ of the Dutch design collective is a shrine to both simplicity and

AKKERMAN

artsiness, with attention-grabbing furniture, clothes and household objects.

GEELS & CO

Warmoesstraat 155. Mon–Sat 9.30am–6pm. MAP PP.34–35, POCKET MAP C11

Oddly situated among Warmoesstraat's loud bars and porn shops, this is one of the city's oldest and best-equipped coffee and tea specialists, and has a small museum of coffee upstairs.

JACOB HOOIJ

Kloveniersburgwal 12. Mon 1–6pm, Tues–Fri 10am–6pm, Sat 10am–5pm. MAP PP.34–35, POCKET MAP C12

In business at this address since 1778, this is a traditional homeopathic chemist with any amount of herbs and natural cosmetics, as well as a huge stock of *drop* (Dutch liquorice).

LAUNDRY INDUSTRY

Spui 1. Mon–Sat 10am–6pm, Thurs until 9pm, Sun noon–6pm. MAP PP.34–35, POCKET MAP B13

Main Amsterdam branch of this cool Dutch womenswear brand: great clothes, and a nice environment for browsing.

P.G.C. HAJENIUS

Rokin 96. Mon noon–6pm, Tues–Sat 9.30am–6pm, Sun noon–5pm. MAP PP.34–35, POCKET MAP B13

Established tobacconist selling its own and other brands of cigars, tobacco, smoking accessories, and every make of cigarette you can think of.

POSTHUMUS

Sint Luciensteeg 23. Mon noon–5pm, Tues–Fri 9am–5pm, Sat 11am–5pm. MAP PP.34–35, POCKET MAP A13

Posh stationery, cards and, best of all, a choice of hundreds of rubber stamps.

PUCCINI

Staalstraat 17. Mon noon–6pm, Tues–Sat 9am–6pm, Sun noon–5pm. MAP PP.34–35, POCKET MAP C14

Perhaps the best chocolate shop in town – all handmade, with an array of fantastic and imaginative fillings.

VROLIJK

Paleisstraat 135. Mon–Fri 11am–6pm, Sat 10am–5pm & Sun 1–5pm. MAP PP.34–35, POCKET MAP A12

The largest gay and lesbian bookshop in Europe, with books, magazines and videos.

Coffeeshops

ABRAXAS

Jonge Roelensteeg 12. Daily 10am–1am. MAP PP.34–35, POCKET MAP B12

Quirky coffeeshop with spiral staircases that are challenging after a spliff. The hot chocolate with hash is not for the susceptible.

DAMPKRING

Handboogstraat 29. Daily 10am–1am. MAP PP.34–35, POCKET MAP A14

Colourful coffeeshop with a laidback atmosphere that is known for its range of good-quality weed and hash. Used as a location in *Ocean's Twelve* starring Brad Pitt.

HILL STREET BLUES

Warmoesstraat 52a. Daily 9am–1am, Fri & Sat until 3am. MAP PP.34–35, POCKET MAP C11

Cosy, graffitied coffeeshop full of comfy chairs and handily situated next door to a police station – hence the name. Also with a smaller sister branch at Nieuwmarkt 14.

KADINSKY

Rosmarijnsteeg 9. Daily 10am–1am, Fri & Sat until 2am. MAP PP.34–35, POCKET MAP A13

Newly renovated, this is the biggest and best of this small chain of coffeeshops, with good deals and excellent hot chocolate.

RUSLAND

Rusland 16. Daily 10am–1am. MAP PP.34–35, POCKET MAP C13

One of the first Amsterdam coffeeshops, a cramped but vibrant place that's a favourite with both dope fans and tea addicts (it has 40 different kinds).

ABRAXAS

47

Cafés and tearooms

CAFÉ BEURS VAN BERLAGE

Beursplein 1. Mon–Sat 10am–7pm, Sun 11am–7pm. MAP PP.34–35, POCKET MAP B12

The best chance to glimpse the interior of the Beurs, and an elegantly furnished place to drink coffee or eat lunch.

DE BIJENKORF KITCHEN

Dam 1. Opening times as for the store (see p.46). MAP PP.34–35 , POCKET MAP B12

Great self-service restaurant that's easily the best spot on Damrak to grab a quick spot of lunch – from sandwiches and burgers to sushi and stir-fries – and a nice environment too, with a small terrace that gives good views of the Oude Kerk tower on fine days (see p.46).

GARTINE

Taksteeg 7 Wed–Sun 10am–6pm. MAP PP.34–35, POCKET MAP B13

Tiny place off one of the grungier stretches of Kalverstraat. Nice breakfasts, an array of inventive sandwiches for lunch, and then – their speciality – high tea served in the afternoon.

HOFJE VAN WIJS

Zeedijk 43. Tues–Sun noon–6pm. MAP PP.34–35, POCKET MAP D11

A hidden treasure in an eighteenth-century courtyard, it sells Indonesian coffee and countless different tea blends.

DE JAREN

Nieuwe Doelenstraat 20. Daily 10am–1am, Fri & Sat until 2am. MAP PP.34–35, POCKET MAP B14

One of the grandest of the grand cafés, overlooking the Amstel next to the university, with three floors and two terraces. A great place to nurse the Sunday papers. It serves reasonably priced food too, and there's a great salad bar.

LATEI

Zeedijk 143. Mon–Wed 8am–6pm, Thurs & Fri 8am–10pm, Sat 9am–10pm, Sun 11am–6pm. MAP PP.34–35, POCKET MAP C12

Homely shop and café that sells bric-a-brac as well as serving good coffee and decent lunches.

PUCCINI

Staalstraat 21. Mon–Fri 8.30am–6pm, Sat & Sun 10am–6pm. MAP PP.34–35, POCKET MAP C14

Lovely café that serves delicious salads, sandwiches and pastries, a few doors down from its sister chocolate shop (see p.65).

VAN BEEREN

Koningstraat 54 Daily 5.30–10.15pm. MAP PP.34–35, POCKET MAP D12

This *eetcafé* serves a satisfying mixture of Dutch staples and modern European fare in relaxed surroundings.

VLAMINCKX

Voetboogstraat 33. Daily noon–6pm. MAP PP.34–35, POCKET MAP A14

Hole-in-the-wall takeaway with a long-established reputation for serving the best *frites* in town.

HOFJE VAN WIJS

Restaurants

BIRD

Zeedijk 77 ☎ 020/420 6289. Daily 1–10pm. MAP PP.34–35, POCKET MAP D11

This Thai canteen is always packed, and rightly so, for its inexpensive and authentic Thai fare. Its big brother across the road serves much the same food in slightly more upscale surroundings.

BLAUWE AAN DE WAAL

Oudezijds Achterburgwal 99 ☎ 020/330 2257. Tues–Sat 6–11pm. MAP PP.34–35, POCKET MAP C12

Quite a haven, situated down an alley in the heart of the Red Light District, with tremendous French-Dutch food and a wonderfully soothing environment after the mayhem of the streets outside.

CAFÉ BERN

Nieuwmarkt 9 ☎ 020/622 0034. Daily 6–11pm. MAP PP.34–35, POCKET MAP D12

Laidback brown café run by a native of Switzerland and patronized by a predominantly arty clientele. Its speciality is, not surprisingly, excellent cheese fondue.

FRENZI

Zwanenburgwal 232 ☎ 020/423.5112. Daily 10am–1am. MAP PP.34–35, POCKET MAP C14

A really busy spot at lunchtime, when it does a stripped-down menu of big sandwiches, salads, soup and a couple of pasta dishes. More upmarket after dark, when its refined and complex regional Italian menu takes over.

HEMELSE MODDER

Oude Waal 11 ☎ 020/624 3203. Daily except Mon 6–11pm. MAP PP.34–35, POCKET MAP D12

Tasty meat, fish and vegetarian food in French-Italian style at reasonable prices in an informal atmosphere. The name "heavenly mud" refers to the dark and white chocolate dessert with vanilla cream.

LUCIUS

Spuistraat 247 ☎ 020/624 1831. Daily 5pm–midnight. MAP PP.34–35, POCKET MAP ??

This bistro-style restaurant, with its high-varnish wooden panelling, is one of the best fish restaurants in town. The lemon sole, when it's on the menu, is particularly excellent. Attracts an older clientele. Mains €25, a tad less for the daily special.

MAPPA

Nes 59 ☎ 020/528 9170. Tues–Sat 6–10pm. MAP PP.34–35, POCKET MAP B13

Classic Italian food with some inventive twists, incorporating good homemade pasta dishes and excellent service in an unpretentious and modern environment.

NAM KEE

Zeedijk 111–113. Daily noon–11pm ☎ 020/624 3470. MAP PP.34–35, POCKET MAP C12

Arguably the best of a number of cheap Chinese diners along this stretch.

DE JAREN

SIE JOE

Gravenstraat 24 ☎ 020/624 1830. Mon–Sat noon–7pm, Thurs until 8pm. MAP PP.34–35, POCKET MAP B12

Small Indonesian café-restaurant whose menu comprises well-prepared, simple dishes such as *gado gado*, *sateh* and *rendang* from €8.25.

VAN KERKWIJK

Nes 41 ☎ 020/620 3316. Daily 11am–late. MAP PP.34–35, POCKET MAP B12

It looks like a bar but is more of a restaurant these days, serving steaks, fish and so on from an ever-changing menu that isn't written down but is heroically memorized by the attentive waiting staff. Good food, and cheap too – mains from €15.

Bars

BAR ITALIA

Rokin 81/Nes 96. Sun–Thurs 10am–3am, Fri & Sat 10am–4am. MAP PP.34–35, POCKET MAP B13

Very popular and ultra-lively bar of the Italian restaurant downstairs. Goes on noisily into the small hours. The restaurant is open until 11pm.

DE BEKEERDE SUSTER

Kloveniersburgwal 6. Mon–Thurs 3pm–1am, Fri & Sat noon–2am, Sun noon–midnight. MAP PP.34–35, POCKET MAP C12

Don't waste your time in the unappealing drinkeries of the Red Light District proper; this place is a few steps away and offers home-brewed beer, a good bar menu and a very convivial atmosphere.

BELGIQUE

Gravenstraat 2. Daily 2pm–1am. MAP PP.34–35, POCKET MAP B12

Tiny bar behind the Nieuwe Kerk that serves up Belgian brews along with sounds from a disc-spinning DJ.

BUBBLES & WINES

Nes 37. Mon–Sat 3.30pm–1am, Sun 2–9pm. MAP PP.34–35, POCKET MAP B12

Over 50 wines by the glass in this elegant wine and champagne bar. The knowledgeable staff will help you decide what to have in line with your tastes.

DE BUURVROUW

St Pieterspoortsteeg 29 Mon–Thurs 10pm–3am, Fri–Sat 10pm–4am. MAP PP.34–35, POCKET MAP B13

Dark, noisy late-night bar with pool, DJs and irregular live music.

DE DRIE FLESCHJES

Gravenstraat 18. Mon–Sat 2–8.30pm, Sun 3–8pm. MAP PP.34–35, POCKET MAP B12

Tasting house for spirits and liqueurs. Clients tend to be well heeled or well soused (often both).

DE ENGELBEWAARDER

Kloveniersburgwal 59. Mon–Thurs 11am–1am, Fri & Sat 11am–3am, Sun 11am–1am. MAP PP.34–35, POCKET MAP C13

Once the meeting place of Amsterdam's bookish types, this is still known as a literary café.

BUBBLES & WINES

It's relaxed and informal, with live jazz on Sunday afternoons.

IN DE WILDEMAN

Kolksteeg 3. Mon–Thurs noon–1am, Fri & Sat noon–2am. MAP PP.34–35, POCKET MAP B11

This lovely old-fashioned bar is housed in a former Amsterdam distillery and offers a huge range of beers (250 and counting) from around the world. A peaceful escape from the loud, tacky shops of nearby Nieuwendijk.

HOPPE

Spui 18. Daily 8am–1am, Fri & Sat until 2am. MAP P.34–35, POCKET MAP A13

One of Amsterdam's oldest and best-known bars, frequented by the city's businessfolk on their way home. Summer is especially good, when the throngs spill out onto the street.

IN 'T AEPJEN

Zeedijk 1. Daily noon–1am. MAP PP.34–35, POCKET MAP C11

A bar since the days when Zeedijk was the haunt of sailors on the razzle, and still one the city centre's best watering holes. Get a plate of cheese or sausage to help the ale go down.

LUXEMBOURG

Spui 24. Daily 9am–1am, Fri & Sat until 2am. MAP PP.34–35, POCKET MAP A13

Crowded, trendy grand café with a long and deep bar, a good selection of snacks, and possibly the best hamburgers in town.

WYNAND FOCKINK

Pijlsteeg 31. Daily 3–9pm. MAP PP.34–35, POCKET MAP B12

Cosy bar hidden just behind the *Krasnapolsky* hotel off Dam Square. It offers a vast range of its own flavoured *jenevers* that used to be distilled down the street.

LUXEMBOURG

Clubs and venues

BITTERZOET

Spuistraat 2 ☎ 020/421 2318, Ⓦ www .bitterzoet.com. Usually Thurs–Sat from 9pm. MAP PP.34–35, POCKET MAP B11

Spacious but cosy two-floored bar and theatre hosting a mixed bag of events: DJ sets, live gigs featuring European indie bands, plus occasional poetry amd film nights.

CLUB NL

Nieuwezijds Voorburgwal 169 ☎ 020/622 7510, Ⓦ www.clubnl.nl. Daily 10pm–3am, Fri & Sat & until 4am. MAP PP.34–35, POCKET MAP A12

What used to be the capital's first lounge bar turned into a stylish house club, frequented by Amsterdam's designer-clad young things.

WINSTON KINGDOM

Warmoesstraat 131 ☎ 020/623 1380, Ⓦ www .winston.nl. Daily 9pm–3am, Fri & Sat until 4am. MAP PP.34–35, POCKET MAP C12

Underground venue in the heart of the Red Light District, hosting everything from DJ nights to band competitions, movie screenings and themed parties.

The Grachtengordel

The Grachtengordel, or "girdle of canals", reaches right round the city centre and is without doubt the most charming part of Amsterdam, its lattice of olive-green waterways and dinky humpback bridges overlooked by street upon street of handsome seventeenth-century canal houses. It's a subtle cityscape – full of surprises, with a bizarre carving here, an unusual facade there, but it is the district's overall atmosphere that appeals rather than any specific sight, with the exception of the Anne Frank Huis. There's no obvious walking route around the Grachtengordel, and you may prefer to wander around as the mood takes you, but the description we've given below goes from north to south, taking in all the highlights on the way. On all three of the main canals – Herengracht, Keizersgracht and Prinsengracht – street numbers begin in the north and increase as you go south.

BROUWERSGRACHT

MAP PP.54–55, POCKET MAP C1–D2

Running east to west along the northern edge of the three main canals is leafy, memorably picturesque **Brouwersgracht**. Originally, Brouwersgracht lay at the edge of Amsterdam's great harbour with easy access to the sea. This was where ships returning from the East unloaded their silks and spices and breweries flourished here too, capitalizing on their ready access to shipments of fresh water. Today, the harbour bustle has moved elsewhere, and the warehouses, with their distinctive spout-neck gables and shuttered windows, formerly used for the delivery and dispatch of goods by pulley from the canal below, have been converted into ritzy apartments that have proved particularly attractive to actors and film producers. There are handsome merchants' houses here as well, plus moored houseboats and a string of quaint little swing bridges. Restaurants have sprung up here too, including one of the city's best, *De Belhamel* (see p.66).

The canals

The canals of the Grachtengordel were dug in the seventeenth century in order to extend the boundaries of a city no longer able to accommodate its burgeoning population. Increasing the area of the city from two to seven square kilometres was a monumental task, and the conditions imposed by the council were strict. The three main waterways – Herengracht, Keizersgracht and Prinsengracht – were set aside for the residences and businesses of the richer and more influential Amsterdam merchants, while the radial cross-streets were reserved for more modest artisans' homes; meanwhile, immigrants, newly arrived to cash in on Amsterdam's booming economy, were assigned, albeit informally, the Jodenhoek (see p.80) and the Jordaan (see p.72). In the Grachtengordel, everyone, even the wealthiest merchant, had to comply with a set of detailed planning regulations. In particular, the council prescribed the size of each building plot – the frontage was set at thirty feet, the depth two hundred – and although there was a degree of tinkering, the end result was the loose conformity you can see today: tall, narrow residences, whose individualism is mainly restricted to the stylistic permutations amongst the **gables**.

The earliest gables,dating from the early seventeenth century, are the so-called **crow-stepped** gables, which were largely superseded by **neck gables** and **bell gables**, both named for the shape of the gable top. Some are embellished, some aren't, many have decorative cornices and the fanciest – which mostly date from the eighteenth century – sport full-scale balustrades. The plainest gables belong to the warehouses, where deep-arched and shuttered windows line up on either side of the loft doors that were once used for loading and unloading goods winched by pulley from the street down below.

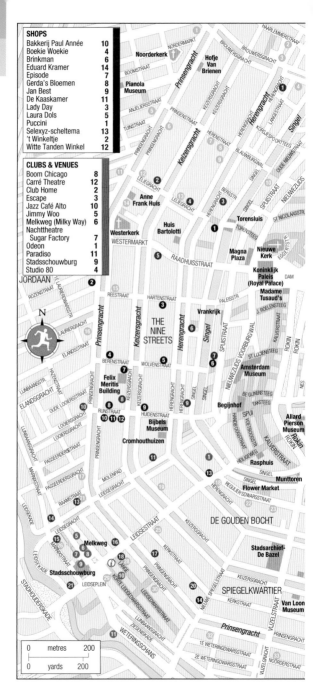

SHOPS

Bakkerij Paul Année	10
Boekie Woekie	4
Brinkman	6
Eduard Kramer	14
Episode	7
Gerda's Bloemen	8
Jan Best	9
De Kaaskamer	11
Lady Day	3
Laura Dols	5
Puccini	1
Selexyz-scheltema	13
't Winkeltje	2
Witte Tanden Winkel	12

CLUBS & VENUES

Boom Chicago	8
Carré Theatre	12
Club Home	2
Escape	3
Jazz Café Alto	10
Jimmy Woo	5
Melkweg (Milky Way)	6
Nachttheatre	
Sugar Factory	7
Odeon	1
Paradiso	11
Stadsschouwburg	9
Studio 80	4

The Grachtengordel

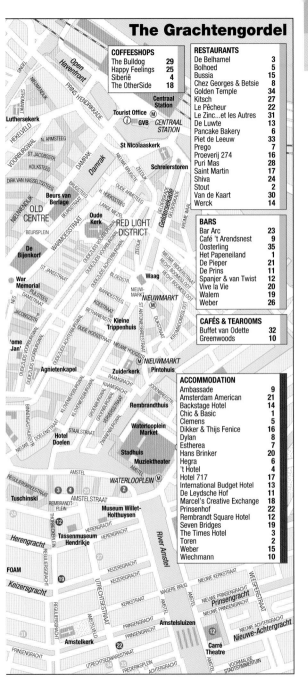

COFFEESHOPS

The Bulldog	29
Happy Feelings	25
Siberië	4
The OtherSide	18

RESTAURANTS

De Belhamel	3
Bolhoed	5
Bussia	15
Chez Georges & Betsie	8
Golden Temple	34
Kitsch	27
Le Pêcheur	22
Le Zinc...et les Autres	31
De Luwte	13
Pancake Bakery	6
Piet de Leeuw	33
Prego	7
Proeverij 274	16
Puri Mas	28
Saint Martin	17
Shiva	24
Stout	2
Van de Kaart	30
Werck	14

BARS

Bar Arc	23
Café 't Arendsnest	9
Oosterling	35
Het Papeneiland	1
De Pieper	21
De Prins	11
Spanjer & van Twist	12
Vive la Vie	20
Walem	19
Weber	26

CAFÉS & TEAROOMS

Buffet van Odette	32
Greenwoods	10

ACCOMMODATION

Ambassade	9
Amsterdam American	21
Backstage Hotel	14
Chic & Basic	1
Clemens	5
Dikker & Thijs Fenice	16
Dylan	8
Estherea	7
Hans Brinker	20
Hegra	6
't Hotel	4
Hotel 717	17
International Budget Hotel	13
De Leydsche Hof	11
Marcel's Creative Exchange	18
Prinsenhof	22
Rembrandt Square Hotel	12
Seven Bridges	19
The Times Hotel	3
Toren	2
Weber	15
Wiechmann	10

HOFJE VAN BRIENEN

Prinsengracht 85–133. Mon–Fri 6am–6pm & Sat 6am–2pm. Free. MAP PP.54–55, POCKET MAP C2

On the east side of Prinsengracht, opposite the Noorderkerk (see p.74), this brown-brick courtyard was built as an almshouse in 1804 by Aernout van Brienen. A well-to-do merchant, Van Brienen had locked himself in his own strongroom by accident and, in a panic, he vowed to build a *hofje* if he was rescued: he was and he did. The plaque inside the complex doesn't give much of the game away, simply inscribed with "For the relief and shelter of those in need."

LELIEGRACHT

MAP PP.54–55, POCKET MAP C3

Leliegracht leads left off Prinsengracht, and is one of the tiny radial canals that cut across the Grachtengordel. It holds one of the city's finest Art Nouveau buildings, a tall and striking building at the Leliegracht-Keizersgracht junction designed by Gerrit van Arkel in 1905. It was originally the headquarters of a life insurance company – hence the two mosaics with angels recommending policies to bemused earthlings.

THE ANNE FRANK HUIS

Prinsengracht 263–267 ☎ 020/556 7100, ⓦ annefrank.org. Mid-March to mid-Sept daily 9am–9pm, Sat till 10pm; July & Aug 9am–10pm; mid-Sept to mid-March daily 9am–7pm, Sat till 9pm; closed Yom Kippur. €9, 10- to 17-year-olds €4.50, under-9s free. Queues can be long, so either come early or book online. MAP PP.54–55, POCKET MAP C3

Easily the city's most visited sight, the **Anne Frank Huis** is where the young diarist and her family hid from the Germans during World War II. Since the posthumous publication of her diaries, Anne Frank has become extraordinarily famous, in the first instance for recording the iniquities of the Holocaust, and latterly as a symbol of the fight against oppression and in particular racism. The family spent over two years in hiding here between 1942 and 1944, but were eventually betrayed and dispatched to Westerbork – the transit camp in the north of the country where most Dutch Jews were processed before being moved to Belsen or Auschwitz. Of the eight souls hidden in the annexe, only Otto Frank survived; Anne and her sister died of typhus within a short time of each other in Belsen, just one

week before the German surrender.

Anne Frank's **diary** was among the few things left behind in the annexe. It was retrieved by one of the people who had helped the Franks and handed to Anne's father on his return from Auschwitz; he later decided to publish it. Since its appearance in 1947, it has been constantly in print and has sold millions of copies.

Despite being so popular, the house has managed to preserve a sense of intimacy, a poignant witness to the personal nature of the Franks' sufferings. The rooms the Franks occupied for two years have been left much the same as they were during the war albeit without the furniture – down to the movie star pin-ups in Anne's bedroom and the marks on the wall recording the children's heights. Video clips of the family in particular and the Holocaust in general give the background. Anne Frank was one of about 100,000 Dutch Jews who died during World War II, and her home provides one of the most enduring testaments to its horrors.

THE WESTERKERK

Prinsengracht 279 ☏ 020/624 7766, ⓦ www.westerkerk.nl. Church: early April to Oct Mon–Sat 11am–3pm, free. Tower: April–Oct Mon–Sat 10am–6pm, €6. MAP PP.54–55, POCKET MAP C3

Trapped in her house, Anne Frank liked to listen to the bells of the **Westerkerk**, just along Prinsengracht, until they were taken away to be melted down for the German war effort. The church still dominates the district, its 85-metre tower – without question Amsterdam's finest – soaring graciously above its surroundings. The church was designed by Hendrick de Keyser and

ENTRANCE TO SECRET ANNEXE AT THE ANNE FRANK HUIS

completed in 1631 as part of the general enlargement of the city, but whereas the exterior is all studied elegance, the interior is bare and plain.

WESTERMARKT

MAP PP.54–55, POCKET MAP C3

Westermarkt, an open square in the shadow of the Westerkerk, possesses two evocative memorials. At the back of the church, beside Keizersgracht, are the three pink granite triangles (one each for the past, present and future) of the **Homomonument**, the world's first memorial to persecuted gays and lesbians, commemorating all those who died at the hands of the Nazis. It was designed by Karin Daan and recalls the pink triangles the Germans made homosexuals sew onto their clothes during World War II.

Nearby, on the south side of the church by Prinsengracht, is a small but beautifully crafted **statue** of Anne Frank by the modern Dutch sculptor Mari Andriessen.

HUIS BARTOLOTTI

Herengracht 170–172. No public access.
MAP PP.54–55, POCKET MAP C3

A brief walk from the Westermarkt, the **Huis Bartolotti** boasts a flashy facade of red brick and stone dotted with urns and columns, faces and shells. The house is an excellent illustration of the Dutch Renaissance style, much more ornate than the typical Amsterdam canal house. The architect was Hendrick de Keyser and a director of the West India Company, Willem van den Heuvel, footed the bill. Van den Heuvel inherited a fortune from his Italian uncle and changed his name in his honour to Bartolotti – hence the name of the house.

WESTERMARKT TO LEIDSEGRACHT – THE NINE STREETS

MAP PP.54–55, POCKET MAP C3–C5

Between Westermarkt and Leidsegracht, the main canals are intercepted by a trio of cross-streets, which are themselves divided into shorter streets that are mostly named after animals whose pelts were once used in the district's tanning industry. There's Reestraat (Deer Street), Hartenstraat (Hart), Berenstraat (Bear) and Wolvenstraat (Wolf), not to mention Huidenstraat (Street of Hides) and Runstraat – a "run" being a bark used in tanning. The tanners are long gone and today these are eminently appealing shopping streets, known as De Negen Straatjes (The Nine Streets).

THE FELIX MERITIS BUILDING

Keizersgracht 324. MAP PP.54–55, POCKET MAP C4

A Neoclassical monolith of 1787, this mansion was built to house the artistic and scientific activities of the eponymous society, which was the cultural focus of the city's upper crust for nearly a hundred years. Dutch cultural aspirations did not, however, impress everyone. It's said that when Napoleon visited the city the entire building was redecorated for his reception, only to have him stalk out in disgust, claiming that the place stank of tobacco. Oddly enough, it later became the headquarters of the Dutch Communist Party, but they sold it to the council who now lease it to the Felix Meritis Foundation for experimental and avant-garde art workshops, conferences, discussions and debates.

HUIS BARTOLOTTI

LEIDSEPLEIN

THE BIJBELS MUSEUM

Herengracht 366–368 ☎ 020/624 2436, ⓦ www.bijbelsmuseum.nl. Mon–Sat 10am–5pm, Sun 11am–5pm. €8. MAP PP.54–55, POCKET MAP C4

The graceful and commanding **Cromhouthuizen**, at Herengracht 364–370, consist of four matching stone mansions, built in the 1660s for one of Amsterdam's wealthy merchant families, the Cromhouts, and two of them now house the **Bijbels Museum**. This contains a splendid selection of old Bibles, including the first Dutch-language Bible ever printed, dating from 1477, and a series of idiosyncratic models of Solomon's Temple and the Jewish Tabernacle, plus a scattering of archeological finds from Palestine and Egypt.

LEIDSEPLEIN

MAP PP.54–55, POCKET MAP C5

Lying on the edge of the Grachtengordel, **Leidseplein** is the bustling hub of Amsterdam's nightlife, a rather cluttered and disorderly open space. The square once marked the end of the road in from Leiden and, as horse-drawn traffic was banned from the centre long ago, it was here that

the Dutch left their horses and carts – a sort of equine car park. Today, it's quite the opposite: continual traffic made up of trams, bikes, cars and pedestrians gives the place a frenetic feel, and the surrounding side streets are jammed with bars, restaurants and clubs in a bright jumble of jutting signs and neon lights. On a good night, Leidseplein can be Amsterdam at its carefree, exuberant best.

STADSSCHOUWBURG

Leidseplein 26 ☎ 020/624 2311, ⓦ www.ssba.nl. MAP PP.54–55, POCKET MAP B5

Leidseplein holds the grandiose **Stadsschouwburg**, a neo-Renaissance edifice dating from 1894, which was so widely criticized for its clumsy vulgarity that the city council of the day temporarily withheld the money for decorating the exterior. Home to the National Ballet and Opera until the Muziektheater (see p.82) was completed on Waterlooplein in 1986, it is now used for theatre, dance and music performances. It also functions as the spot where the Ajax football team gather on the balcony to wave to the crowds whenever they win anything, as they often do.

59

LEIDSESTRAAT

MAP PP.54–55, POCKET MAP C5

Heading northeast from Leidseplein, **Leidsestraat** is a crowded shopping street that leads across the three main canals up towards the Singel and the flower market (see p.63). En route, at the corner of Keizersgracht, is the **Metz & Co** department store, which was, when it was built, the tallest commercial building in the city – one reason why the owners were able to entice Gerrit Rietveld, the leading architectural light of the De Stijl movement, to add a rooftop glass and metal showroom in 1933. The showroom has survived and is now a café offering one of the best views over the centre in this predominantly low-rise city.

THE SPIEGELKWARTIER

MAP PP.54–55, POCKET MAP C6

South of Metz & Co, along Keizersgracht, is **Nieuwe Spiegelstraat**, an appealing mixture of bookshops and corner cafés that extends south into Spiegelgracht to form the Spiegelkwartier – home to the pricey end of Amsterdam's antiques trade.

DE GOUDEN BOCHT

MAP PP.54–55, POCKET MAP D5

Nieuwe Spiegelstraat meets the elegant sweep of Herengracht near the west end of the so-called De Gouden Bocht (the **Golden Bend**), where the canal is overlooked by double-fronted mansions – some of the most opulent dwellings in the city. Most of these houses were remodelled in the late seventeenth and eighteenth centuries. Characteristically, they have double stairways leading to the entrance, underneath which the small door was for the servants, while up above, the majority of the houses are topped off by the ornamental cornices that were fashionable at the time. Classical references are common, both in form – pediments, columns and pilasters – and decoration, from scrolls and vases through to geometric patterns inspired by ancient Greece.

THE STADSARCHIEF – DE BAZEL

Vijzelstraat 32 ☎ 020/251 1510, ⓦ www .stadsarchief.amsterdam.nl. Tues–Fri 10am–5pm, Sat & Sun noon–5pm. Free. MAP PP.54–55, POCKET MAP D5

Stretching down Vijzelstraat from Herengracht is one of

Amsterdam's most incongruous buildings – you can't possibly miss its looming, geometrical brickwork. Now home to the **Stadsarchief**, the state archives, it started out as the headquarters of a Dutch shipping company, the Nederlandsche Handelsmaatschappij, before falling into the hands of the ABN-AMRO bank, which was itself swallowed by a consortium led by the Royal Bank of Scotland in 2007. Dating to the 1920s, the building is known as **De Bazel** after the architect Karel de Bazel (1869–1923), whose devotion to theosophy – a combination of metaphysics and religious philosophy – formed and framed his design. Every facet of Bazel's building reflects the theosophical desire for order and balance from the pink and yellow brickwork of the exterior (representing male and female respectively) to the repeated use of motifs drawn from the Middle East, the source of much of the cult's spiritual inspiration. At the heart of the building is the Schatkamer (Treasury), an Art Deco extravagance that exhibits an intriguing selection of photographs and documents drawn from the city's vast archives.

THE TASSENMUSEUM HENDRIKJE (PURSE & BAG MUSEUM)

Herengracht 573 ☎ 020/524 6452, ⓦ www .tassenmuseum.nl. Daily 10am–5pm. €8.50. MAP PP.54–55, POCKET MAP E5

This delightful museum holds a superb collection of handbags, pouches, wallets, bags and purses from medieval times onwards, exhibited on three floors of a grand old mansion. The collection begins on the top floor with a curious miscellany of items from the sixteenth to the nineteenth centuries. The next floor down focuses on the twentieth century, with several beautiful Art Nouveau handbags, while the final floor is given over to temporary displays.

THE MUSEUM WILLET-HOLTHUYSEN

Herengracht 605 ☎ 020/523 1822, ⓦ www .museumwilletholthuysen.nl. Mon–Fri 10am–5pm, Sat & Sun 11am–5pm. €8. MAP PP.54–55, POCKET MAP E5

The coal-trading Holthuysen family occupied this elegant, mansion until the last of the line, Sandra Willet-Holthuysen, gifted her home and its contents to the city in 1895. The most striking room is the **Blue Room**, which has been returned to its original eighteenth-century Rococo appearance – a flashy and ornate style that the Dutch merchants of the day regarded as the epitome of refinement and good taste. Other rooms have the more cluttered appearance of the nineteenth century and the house also displays a small collection of glass, silver, majolica and ceramics assembled by Sandra's husband, Abraham Willet.

THE AMSTEL AND THE MAGERE BRUG

MAP PP.54–55, POCKET MAP E5–G9 & F6

The Grachtengordel comes to an abrupt halt at the River Amstel. The **Magere Brug** (Skinny Bridge), spanning the Amstel at the end of Kerkstraat, is the most famous and arguably the cutest of the city's many swing bridges. Legend has it that this bridge, which dates back to about 1670, replaced an even older and skinnier version, originally built by two sisters who lived on either side of the river and were fed up with having to walk so far to see each other.

THE AMSTELSLUIZEN

MAP PP.54–55, POCKET MAP F6

The **Amstelsluizen** – or Amstel locks – are closed every night when the council begin the process of sluicing out the canals. A huge pumping station on an island out to the east of the city then starts to pump fresh water from the IJsselmeer into the canal system; similar locks on the west side of the city are left open for the surplus to flow into the IJ and, from there, out to sea. The watery content of the canals is thus regularly refreshed – though, despite this, and with three centuries of algae, prams, shopping trolleys and a few hundred rusty bikes, the water is only appealing as long as you're not actually in it.

THE AMSTELVELD AND REGULIERSGRACHT

MAP PP.54–55, POCKET MAP D5

Doubling back from the Amstel Sluizen, turn left along the north side of Prinsengracht and you soon reach the **Amstelveld**, where the Monday **flower market** sells flowers and plants, and is much less of a scrum than the Bloemenmarkt (see opposite). Adjacent **Reguliers -gracht** is one of the three surviving radial canals that cut across the Grachtengordel, its dainty humpback bridges and sparkling waters overlooked by charming seventeenth- and eighteenth-century canal houses.

FOAM

Keizersgracht 609 ☎ 020/551 6500, ⓦ www .foam.org. Daily 10am–6pm, Thurs & Fri until 9pm. €8.50. MAP PP.54–55, POCKET MAP D5

Located right on the canal, this four-storey museum of photography breathes history on the outside, but has a modern and industrial feel once you enter. **FOAM** aims to be a platform for both well-established photographers and young and upcoming talent, providing them with an opportunity to reach a larger audience. All genres of photography are covered and exhibitions are rotated regularly, with opening days often attracting hundreds of enthusiasts. Recent exhibitions have included the abstractions of Michael Wolf, the controversial Ari Marcopoulos and Cuny Janssen's whimsical My Grandma was a Turtle.

MUSEUM VAN LOON

MUSEUM VAN LOON

Keizersgracht 672 ☎ 020/624 5255, ⓦ www
.museumvanloon.nl. Daily except Tues
11am–5pm. €10. MAP PP.54–55, POCKET MAP D6

The **Museum Van Loon** boasts
the finest accessible canal house
interior in Amsterdam. Built in
1672, and first occupied by the
artist and pupil of Rembrandt,
Ferdinand Bol, the house has
been returned to something
akin to its eighteenth-century
appearance, with acres of wood
panelling and fancy stucco
work. Look out also for the
ornate copper balustrade on
the staircase, into which is
worked the name "Van
Hagen-Trip" (after a one-time
owner of the house); the Van
Loons later filled the spaces
between the letters with iron
curlicues to prevent their
children falling through. The
top-floor landing has several
paintings sporting Roman
figures, and one of the
bedrooms – the "painted room"
– is decorated with a Romantic
painting of Italy, a favourite
motif in Amsterdam from
around 1750 to 1820. The
oddest items are the fake
bedroom doors: the
eighteenth-century owners
were so keen to avoid any lack
of symmetry that they
camouflaged the real bedroom
doors and created imitation,
decorative doors in the
"correct" position instead.

REMBRANDTPLEIN

MAP PP.54–55, POCKET MAP E5

One of the larger open spaces
in the city centre,
Rembrandtplein is a neat and
trim open space that was
formerly Amsterdam's butter
market. It was renamed in
1876, and is today one of the
city's nightlife centres,
although its crowded
restaurants and bars are firmly
tourist-targeted. Rembrandt's
statue stands in the middle, his
back wisely turned against the
square's worst excesses,
though, to be fair, the *Hotel
Schiller*, with its Art Deco
flourishes, does provide some
architectural flair.

THE MUNTTOREN AND
BLOEMENMARKT (FLOWER
MARKET)

MAP PP.54–55, POCKET MAP D5

Tiny Muntplein is dominated
by the **Munttoren**, an imposing
fifteenth-century tower that
was once part of the old city
wall. Later, the tower was
adopted as the municipal mint
– hence its name – and
Hendrik de Keyser, in one of
his last commissions, added a
flashy spire in 1620. A few
metres away, the floating
Bloemenmarkt, or **flower
market** (daily 9am–5pm, some
stalls close on Sun), extends
along the southern bank of the
Singel. Popular with locals and
tourists alike, the market is one
of the main suppliers of flowers
to central Amsterdam, but its
blooms and bulbs now share
stall space with souvenir clogs,
garden gnomes, Delftware and
similar tat.

Shops

BAKKERIJ PAUL ANNÉE

Runstraat 25. Mon–Fri 8am–6pm & Sat 8am–5pm & Sun 10am–3pm. MAP PP.54–55, POCKET MAP C4

The best wholegrain and sourdough breads in town, bar none, all made from organic grains.

BOEKIE WOEKIE

Berenstraat 16. Daily noon–6pm. MAP PP.54–55, POCKET MAP C4

Sells books on – and by – leading Dutch artists and graphic designers, and entertaining postcards too.

BRINKMAN

Singel 319. Mon–Fri 10am–5pm & Sat 11am–5pm. MAP PP.54–55, POCKET MAP D4

A stalwart of the Amsterdam antiquarian book trade, *Brinkman* has lots of good local stuff with expert advice if and when you need it.

EDUARD KRAMER

Nieuwe Spiegelstraat 64. Tues–Sat 10am–6pm, Mon & Sun 1–6pm. MAP PP.54–55, POCKET MAP C6

Holds a wonderful selection of Dutch tiles from the fifteenth century onwards; it also operates an online ordering service.

EPISODE

Berenstraat 1. Mon & Sun 1–6pm, Tues–Wed 11am–6pm, Thurs 11am–8pm, Fri 11am–7pm, Sat 10am–7pm. MAP PP.54–55, POCKET MAP C4

One of the larger secondhand stores, with everything from army jackets to hats, fur coats, shoes and belts. Specializes in the 1970s and 1980s.

GERDA'S BLOEMEN

Runstraat 16. Mon–Fri 9am–6pm & Sat 9am–5pm. MAP PP.54–55 ,POCKET MAP C4

Amsterdam is full of flower shops, but this one is the most imaginative and sensual. Bouquets to melt the hardest of hearts.

JAN BEST

Keizersgracht 357, corner Huidenstraat. Tues–Sat noon–6pm & Sun noon–5pm 1.30–5pm. MAP PP.54–55, POCKET MAP C4

Famed antique lamp shop, with some wonderfully kitsch examples as well as offbeat new lamps and lights.

DE KAASKAMER

Runstraat 7. Mon noon–6pm, Tues–Fri 9am–6pm, Sat 9am–5pm & Sun noon–5pm. MAP PP.54–55, POCKET MAP C4

Friendly shop with a comprehensive selection of Dutch cheeses – much more than ordinary Edam – plus olives and international wines.

LADY DAY

Hartenstraat 9. Mon–Sat 11am–6pm, Thurs until 9pm & Sun 1–6pm. MAP PP.54–55, POCKET MAP C3

Good-quality secondhand clothes with the emphasis on

LAURA DOLS

1960s and 1970s. Strong on suits and vintage dresses.

LAURA DOLS

Wolvenstraat 6 & 7. Mon–Sat 11am–6pm Thurs until 9pm & Sun 1–6pm. MAP PP.54–55, POCKET MAP C4

Superb – and superbly creative – assortment of vintage clothing from dresses through to hats. Its forte is 1940s and 1950s gear.

PUCCINI

Singel 184, junction of Oude Leliestraat, Ⓦwww.puccinibomboni.com. Mon noon–6pm, Tues–Sat 11am–6pm & Sun noon–5pm. MAP PP.54–55, POCKET MAP A11

Without doubt the best chocolatier in town, selling a wonderfully creative range of chocs in all sorts of shapes and sizes. This mini-chain has also abandoned the tweeness of the traditional chocolatier for brisk modern decor. Also at Staalstraat 17 (see p.47).

SELEXYZ-SCHELTEMA

Koningsplein 20. Mon–Sat 10am–6pm, Thurs until 9pm & Sun noon–6pm. MAP PP.54–55, POCKET MAP C5

Amsterdam's biggest and best bookshop. Six floors of absolutely everything and although most of the books are in Dutch, there are good English sections too.

'T WINKELTJE

Prinsengracht 228. Mon 1–5.30pm, Tues–Fri 10am–5.30pm & Sat 10am–5pm. MAP PP.54–55, POCKET MAP C3

A jumble of bargain-basement glassware and crockery, candlesticks, antique tin toys, kitsch souvenirs, old apothecaries' jars and flasks. Perfect for browsing.

WITTE TANDENWINKEL

Runstraat 5. Mon 1–6pm, Tues–Fri 10am–6pm & Sat 10am–5pm. MAP PP.54–55, POCKET MAP C4

The "White Teeth Shop" sells wacky toothbrushes and just about every dental hygiene accoutrement you could ever need.

Coffeeshops

THE BULLDOG

Leidseplein 15. Daily 10am–1am, 3am at weekends. MAP PP.54–55, POCKET MAP C5

The biggest and most famous of the coffeeshop chains, and a long way from its poky Red Light District-dive origins. This, the main Leidseplein branch (the Palace), housed in a former police station, has a large cocktail bar, coffeeshop, juice bar and souvenir shop, all with separate entrances. It's big and brash, not at all the place for a quiet smoke, though the dope they sell (packaged up in neat little brand-labelled bags) is reliably good.

HAPPY FEELINGS

Kerkstraat 51. Daily 1pm–1am. MAP PP.54–55, POCKET MAP C5

What used to be a hippie hangout, turned into a fresh and trendy coffeeshop with flatscreens on the walls, attracting a select clientele.

SIBERIË

Brouwersgracht 11. Daily 11am–11pm. MAP
PP.54–55, POCKET MAP B10
Very relaxed, very friendly, and
worth a visit whether you want
to smoke or not.

THE OTHERS IDE

Reguliersdwarsstraat 6. Daily 11am–1am.
MAP PP.54–55, POCKET MAP A14
Essentially a gay coffeeshop (in
Dutch, "the other side" is a
euphemism for gay), but
straight-friendly and with a fun
atmosphere.

BUSSIA

Cafés and tearooms

BUFFET VAN ODETTE

Prinsengracht 598. Sun & Mon 10am–5pm,
Wed–Sat 10am–8.30pm, closed Tues. MAP
PP.54–55, POCKET MAP A13
Smart, modern and attractive
café serving excellent light
meals and salads, plus more
substantial meals in the
evening. The fresh pasta dishes
are especially good (from €12).

GREENWOODS

Singel 103. Mon–Thurs 9.30am–5pm, Fri–Sun
9.30am–6pm. MAP PP.54–55, POCKET MAP B11
Cosy English-style teashop
in the basement of a canal
house. Pies and sandwiches,
pots of tea – and a decent
breakfast.

Restaurants

DE BELHAMEL

Brouwersgracht 60 ☎ 020/622 1095. Daily
noon–4pm & 6–10pm. MAP PP.54–55, POCKET
MAP B10
Smashing restaurant where the
Art Nouveau decor makes for a
delightful setting and the menu
is short but extremely

well-chosen, mixing Dutch
with French dishes. Main
courses at around €20–25.

BOLHOED

Prinsengracht 60 ☎ 020/626 1803. Daily
noon–10pm. MAP PP.54–55, POCKET MAP C2
Something of an Amsterdam
institution, the daily changing
menu here features familiar
vegan and vegetarian options,
with organic beer to wash it
down. Mains at around €15.

BUSSIA

Reestraat 28 ☎ 020/627 8794. Daily noon–3pm
& 6–10.30pm. MAP PP.54–55, POCKET MAP C3
Top notch Italian restaurant
with fresh ingredients.
Everything is homemade, from
the original Italian *gelato* to the
pasta. Many wines per glass.
Mains around €25, a bit less for
pasta.

CHEZ GEORGES & BETSIE

Herenstraat 3 ☎ 020/626 3332. Daily except
Wed & Sun 6–11pm. MAP PP.54–55, POCKET
MAP A11
This much-lauded restaurant
offers immaculately presented
dishes from a well-chosen
menu. The old fashioned
interior adds to the homely
feel. Main courses cost €23 and

up, though you might prefer the three-course set menu instead. Has an excellent selection of wines, too.

GOLDEN TEMPLE

Utrechtsestraat 126 ☎ 020/626 8560. Daily 5–9.30pm. MAP PP.54–55, POCKET MAP E6

Laidback place with a little more soul than the average Amsterdam veggie joint. Pleasant, attentive service. No alcohol.

KITSCH

Utrechtsestraat 42 ☎ 020/625 9251. Tues–Sat 6–11pm. MAP PP.54–55, POCKET MAP E6

Exuberant flower power in this retro restaurant with old movies projected on the wall and cushions in every thinkable design. The menu is less adventurous, ranging from a simple hamburger to lobster, at reasonable prices.

LE PÊCHEUR

Reguliersdwarsstraat 32 ☎ 020/624 3121. Mon–Sat 5.30–10.30pm. MAP PP.54–55, POCKET MAP A14

Seafood restaurant with a well-considered menu, both set menus and à la carte, with mains around €23.

LE ZINC ... ET LES AUTRES

Prinsengracht 999 ☎ 020/622 9044. Mon–Sat 5.30–11pm. MAP PP.54–55, POCKET MAP D6

Atmospheric little place serving good-quality, sophisticated dishes, such as veal with artichoke or tuna steak and feta salad, averaging €28; there's a good wine list too.

DE LUWTE

Leliegracht 26 ☎ 020/625 8548. Daily 6–10pm. MAP PP.54–55, POCKET MAP A11

This cordial restaurant is kitted out with yellow tables and pastel walls embellished with Art Nouveau flourishes. The small but well-chosen menu offers Dutch/Mediterranean cuisine – the seafood is delicious. Mains from €20.

PANCAKE BAKERY

Prinsengracht 191 ☎ 020/625 1333. Daily noon–9.30pm. MAP PP.54–55, POCKET MAP C2

Located in the basement of an old canal house, this restaurant offers a mind-boggling range of fillings for its pancakes (€8–14), from classic ham and cheese to Thai red curry.

PIET DE LEEUW

Noorderstraat 11 ☎ 020/623 7181. Mon–Fri noon–11pm, Sat & Sun 5–11pm; closed for summer holidays two weeks in August. MAP PP.54–55, POCKET MAP D6

Arguably Amsterdam's best steakhouse, an old-fashioned, darkly lit, wood-panelled affair dating back to the 1940s. Doubles as a local bar, but the steaks, served every which way and costing around €17, are excellent.

PREGO

Herenstraat 25 ☎ 020/638 0148. Daily 6–10pm. MAP PP.54–55, POCKET MAP D2

Informal French-Mediterranean restaurant with modern decor offering tasty dishes such as *coq au vin*, *bouillabaisse* and red sea bass with couscous. Mains average €22.

PANCAKE BAKERY

PROEVERIJ 274

Prinsengracht 274 ☎ 020/421 1848. Daily 6–10pm. MAP PP.54–55. POCKET MAP C4

Cosy split-level restaurant with sixteenth-century relics on the wall and a first-class menu offering classic dishes with a modern twist. Solely organic meat and fish in season. Mains from €25.

PURI MAS

Lange Leidsedwarsstraat 37 ☎ 020/627 7627. Daily from 6–11pm. MAP PP.54–55. POCKET MAP C5

Exceptionally good value Indonesian, on a street better known for rip-offs. Friendly and informed service preludes spectacular *rijsttafels*, both meat and vegetarian.

SAINT MARTIN

Prinsengracht 358 ☎ 020/620 2757. Wed–Sun 4–10pm. MAP PP.54–55. POCKET MAP C5

Cheerful little place offering Mediterranean cuisine with only the freshest of ingredients in an informal setting. Attractively located on the canal side.

SHIVA

Reguliersdwarsstraat 72 ☎ 020/624 8713. Daily 5–11pm. MAP PP.54–55. POCKET MAP D5

Competent Indian restaurant in terms of quality and price, with a wide selection of dishes, all expertly prepared and moderately priced.

STOUT

Haarlemmerstraat 73 ☎ 020/616 3664. Daily 10am–11pm, Sun from 11am. MAP PP.54–55. POCKET MAP D1

Lively and fashionable café restaurant, popular with locals. Great sandwiches and salads at daytime and everything from duck to fresh oysters in the evening. Comfortable velvet lounge seats outside make it a great spot to linger.

VAN DE KAART

Prinsengracht 512 ☎ 020/625 9232. Mon–Sat 5.30–10.30pm. MAP PP.54–55. POCKET MAP C6

Slick and chic restaurant, with an enterprising French-inspired menu including poached lobster, smoked mackerel and beef cheek stew-stuffed ravioli. Excellent wine list.

WERCK

Prinsengracht 277 ☎ 020/627 4079. ⓦ www .werck.nl. Tues–Sat 5–11pm. MAP PP.54–55. POCKET MAP C3

Located right next to the Anne Frank Huis, this smart place offers flavoursome mains like pan-fried John Dory and venison stew for around €25. Turns into a lively place with DJs at night.

Bars

BAR ARC

Reguliardwarsstraat 44. Daily 4pm–1am, Fri & Sat until 3am. MAP PP.54–55. POCKET MAP D5

Huge and fashionable gay spot, with fluorescent pink lights and multiple bars. Cocktail nights and DJs on weekends. Also frequented by non-gays.

CAFÉ 'T ARENDSNEST

Herengracht 90. Mon–Thurs 4pm–midnight, Friday 4pm–2am, Sat 2pm–2am & Sun 2–11.30pm. MAP PP.54–55, POCKET MAP D2

In a handsome old canal house, this bar boasts impressive wooden decor – from the longest of bars to the tall wood-and-glass cabinets – and specializes in Dutch beers, of which it has 130 varieties.

OOSTERLING

Utrechtsestraat 140. Mon–Sat noon–1am, Sun 1–8pm. MAP PP.54–55, POCKET MAP E6

Stone-floored, neighbourhood bar-cum-off-licence that's been owned by the same family for years. Kitted out in traditional style, it specializes in *jenever* (gin) with dozens of brands and varieties.

HET PAPENEILAND

Prinsengracht 2. Daily 10am–1am, Fri & Sat until 3am. MAP PP.54–55, POCKET MAP D1

With its wood panelling, antique Delft tiles and ancient stove, this is one of the cosiest bars in the Grachtengordel, though it does get packed late at night with a garrulous crew.

DE PIEPER

Prinsengracht 424. Mon–Thurs 11am–1am, Fri & Sat until 2am. MAP PP.54–55, POCKET MAP C5

Relaxed neighbourhood brown bar with rickety old furniture and a terrace beside the canal.

DE PRINS

Prinsengracht 124. Daily 10am–1am. MAP PP.54–55, POCKET MAP C3

With its well-worn decor and chatty atmosphere, this popular and lively brown bar offers a wide range of drinks and well-priced food, served 10am–10pm.

SPANJER & VAN TWIST

Leliegracht 60. Daily 10am–10pm; Lunch served daily 10am–4pm, evening meals 6–10pm. MAP PP.54–55, POCKET MAP C2

Café-bar with an arty air and brisk modern fittings. Tasty snacks and light meals plus an outside mini-terrace right on the canal.

VIVE LA VIE

Amstelstraat 7. Daily 4pm–1am, Fri & Sat until 3am. MAP PP.54–55, POCKET MAP E5

Small, campy bar, patronized mostly, but not exclusively, by women and transvestites. Quiet during the week, it steams on the weekend.

WALEM

Keizersgracht 449. Mon & Tues 9.30am–7pm, Wed–Sun 9.30am–10.30pm. MAP PP.54–55, POCKET MAP C5

A chic café-bar – cool, light and with a stylish clientele. The food is hybrid Mediterranean-Eastern. Breakfast in the garden during the summer is a highlight. Usually packed.

WEBER

Marnixstraat 397. Daily 9pm–3am, Fri & Sat until 4am. MAP PP.54–55, POCKET MAP B5

Popular local hangout attracting musicians, students and young professionals. Crowded at the weekends but friendly.

SPANJER & VAN TWIST

Clubs and venues

BOOM CHICAGO

Leidseplein 12 ☎ 020/423 0101, ⓦ www
.boomchicago.nl. MAP PP.54–55, POCKET MAP C5
Something of a phenomenon in
Amsterdam, this rapid-fire
improv comedy troupe hailing
from the US performs at the
Leidseplein Theater nightly to
crowds of both tourists and
locals alike. With inexpensive
food, cocktails and beer served
in pitchers, the comedy need
not be funny – but it is.

JAZZ CAFÉ ALTO

Korte Leidsedwarsstraat 115 ☎ 020/626
3249, ⓦ www.jazz-cafe-alto.nl. Daily
9pm–3am. MAP PP.54–55, POCKET MAP C5
It's worth hunting down this
legendary little jazz bar just off
Leidseplein for its quality
modern jazz. It's big on
atmosphere, though slightly
cramped, and entry is free.

CARRÉ THEATRE

Amstel 115–125 ☎ 020/524 9452, ⓦ www
.carre.nl. MAP PP.54–55, POCKET MAP F6
A splendid late-nineteenth
-century structure comprises

the ultimate venue for Dutch
folk artists, and hosts all kinds
of top international acts –
anything from Van Morrison
to Carmen, with reputable
touring orchestras and opera
companies squeezed in
between.

CLUB HOME

Wagenstraat 3 ☎ 020/620 1375, ⓦ www
.clubhome.nl. Thurs 11pm–4am, Fri & Sat
10pm–5am. MAP PP.54–55, POCKET MAP E5
Relaxed dance club, divided
over three floors offering all
styles of house and club
music. Mixed audience with
mainly students on Thursday
and the hip and creative on
weekends.

ESCAPE

Rembrandtplein 11 ☎ 020/622 1111, ⓦ www
.escape.nl. Thurs–Sun 11pm–4/5am. MAP
PP.54–55, POCKET MAP E5
This vast club has space enough
to house 2000 people, but its
glory days – when it was home
to Amsterdam's cutting edge
Chemistry nights – are long
gone and it now focuses on
weekly club nights that pull in
crowds of mainstream punters.
The opening of the *Escape* café,
lounge and studio should pull
in more trendsetting crowds
though.

JIMMY WOO

Korte Leidsedwarsstraat 18 ☎ 020/626 3150,
ⓦ www.jimmywoo.com. Thurs–Sun
11pm–3/4am. MAP PP.54–55, POCKET MAP B5
Intimate and stylish club spread
over two floors. Upstairs, the
black lacquered walls, Japanese
lamps and cosy booths with
leather couches ooze sexy chic,
while downstairs a packed
dance floor throbs under
hundreds of oscillating
lightbulbs studded into the
ceiling. Popular with young,
well-dressed locals so look
smart if you want to join in.

MELKWEG (MILKY WAY)

Lijnbaansgracht 234a ☎ 020/531 8181, ⓦ www.melkweg.nl. Wed–Sat from 8pm. MAP PP.54–55, POCKET MAP C5

Probably Amsterdam's most famous entertainment venue. A former dairy (hence the name) just round the corner from Leidseplein, this has two separate halls for live music, and puts on a broad range of bands covering everything from reggae to rock, all of which lean towards the "alternative". Excellent DJ sessions go on late at the weekend. There's also a monthly film programme, a theatre, gallery and café-restaurant (Marnixstraat entrance).

ODEON

Singel 460 ☎ 020/521 8555, ⓦ www.odeontheater.nl. Club Fri & Sat 11pm–5am; restaurant Fri & Sat from 6pm. MAP PP.54–55, POCKET MAP D5

Originally a brewery dating from 1662, this restored canal house has since been a theatre, cinema and concert hall until it was gutted in a fire in 1990. Rescued, it's now a stylish nightclub and restaurant. The club takes up the old ballroom and has a vast dancefloor overlooked by balconies, perfect for people-watching.

PARADISO

Weteringschans 6–8 ☎ 020/626 8790, ⓦ www.paradiso.nl. MAP PP.54–55, POCKET MAP C6

A converted church near the Leidseplein, revered by many for its excellent programme, featuring local and international bands. Club nights such as Noodlanding! draw in the crowds, and look out also for DJ sets on Saturdays. Sometimes hosts classical concerts, as well as debates and multimedia events.

ODEON

STADSSCHOUWBURG

Leidseplein 26 ☎ 020/624 2311, ⓦ www.ssba.nl. MAP PP.54–55, POCKET MAP C6

Long-established concert hall in the thick of Amsterdam's nightlife offering a wide range of performances, including theatre, opera and dance by both Dutch and foreign troupes. Discount tickets available for under-30s.

STUDIO 80

Rembrandtplein 17 ☎ 020/521 8333, ⓦ www.studio-80.nl. Wed–Sat from 10pm. MAP PP.54–55, POCKET MAP E5

Right on the Rembrandtplein, this place celebrates the underground scene with techno, soul, funk, minimal and electro. A breeding ground for upcoming DJs and bands.

NACHTTHEATRE SUGAR FACTORY

Lijnbaansgracht 238 ☎ 020/627 0008, ⓦ www.sugarfactory.nl. Nightly except Mon & Tues. MAP PP.54–55, POCKET MAP C5

This distinctive "theatrical nightclub" on busy Leidseplein hosts a programme of cabaret, live music, poetry and theatre, plus a late-night club that kicks off after the show. Pulls in a young and artistic crowd.

The Jordaan and Western docklands

On the western side of the city centre, the Jordaan is an area of slender canals and narrow streets flanked by an agreeable mix of modest, modern terraces and handsome seventeenth-century canal houses. It was traditionally the home of Amsterdam's working class, but in recent decades it has become one of the most sought-after residential neighbourhoods in the city. Until the 1970s, the inhabitants were primarily stevedores and factory workers earning a crust in the Scheepvaartsbuurt (Shipping Quarter) that edges the north of the Jordaan. This is now a mixed shopping and residential quarter, while just beyond, the Westerdok is the oldest part of the sprawling complex of artificial islands that today sweeps along the south side of the River IJ.

THE JORDAAN

MAP P.73, POCKET MAP B3

According to dyed-in-the-wool locals, the true Jordaaner is born within earshot of the Westerkerk bells, which means that there are endless arguments as to quite where the district's southern boundary lies, though at least the other borders are clear – Prinsengracht, Brouwersgracht and Lijnbaansgracht.

The streets just north of Leidsegracht – generally deemed to be the southern border – are routinely modern, though **Looiersgracht**, running either side of its canal, does have its scenic moments. A few blocks further north, the area's artery, **Rozengracht**, slices through the centre of the Jordaan, though this wide street lost most of its character when its canal was filled in and is now a busy main road. It was here, at no. 184, that

Rembrandt spent the last ten years of his life in diminished circumstances – a scrolled plaque distinguishes his old home.

ANTIQUES AT DE LOOIER

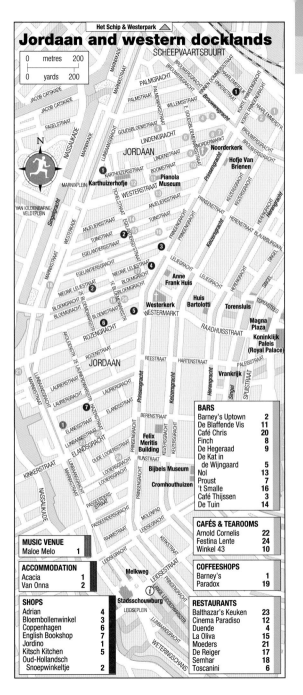

Jordaan and western docklands

MUSIC VENUE

Maloe Melo	1

ACCOMMODATION

Acacia	1
Van Onna	2

SHOPS

Adrian	4
Bloembollenwinkel	3
Coppenhagen	6
English Bookshop	7
Jordino	1
Kitsch Kitchen	5
Oud-Hollandsch Snoepwinkeltje	2

BARS

Barney's Uptown	2
De Blaffende Vis	11
Café Chris	20
Finch	8
De Hegeraad	9
De Kat in de Wijngaard	5
Nol	13
Proust	7
't Smalle	16
Café Thijssen	3
De Tuin	14

CAFÉS & TEAROOMS

Arnold Cornelis	22
Festina Lente	24
Winkel 43	10

COFFEESHOPS

Barney's	1
Paradox	19

RESTAURANTS

Balthazar's Keuken	23
Cinema Paradiso	12
Duende	4
La Oliva	15
Moeders	21
De Reiger	17
Semhar	18
Toscanini	6

ROZENGRACHT TO WESTERSTRAAT

MAP P.73, POCKET MAP B3 & B2-C2

The streets and canals between Rozengracht and Westerstraat form the heart of the Jordaan and hold the district's prettiest sights. North of Rozengracht, the first canal is the **Bloemgracht** (Flower Canal), a leafy waterway dotted with houseboats and arched by dinky little bridges, its network of cross-streets sprinkled with cafés, bars and idiosyncratic shops. A narrow cross-street, **2e Egelantiersdwarsstraat** – and its continuation **2e Tuindwarsstraat** and **2e Anjeliersdwarsstraat** – runs north from Bloemgracht flanked by many of the Jordaan's more fashionable stores and clothing shops, as well as some of its liveliest bars and cafés. At the end is workaday **Westerstraat**, a busy modern thoroughfare dotted with more mainstream shops.

PIANOLA MUSEUM

Westerstraat 106 ☎ 020/627 9624, Ⓦ www .pianola.nl. Sun 2–5pm. €5. MAP P.73, POCKET MAP C2

This small but charming museum has a collection of **pianolas** and automatic music

machines dating from the beginning of the twentieth century, fifteen of which have been restored to working order. These machines were the jukeboxes of their day, and the museum has a vast collection of over 15,000 rolls of music, some of which were "recorded" by famous pianists and composers – Gershwin, Debussy, Scott Joplin and others. It also runs a regular programme of pianola music concerts (check their website).

THE NOORDERKERK

Noorderkermarkt ☎ 020/626 6436, Ⓦ www .noorderkerk.org. Mon 10.30am–12.30pm, Sat 11am–1pm & April–Oct Sun 1.30–5.30pm. Free. MAP P.73, POCKET MAP C2

Hendrik de Keyser's last creation, finished two years after his death in 1623, this bulky brick building represented a radical departure from the conventional church designs of the time, having a symmetrical Greek-cross floor plan, with four arms radiating out from a steepled centre. Uncompromisingly dour, it proclaimed the serious intent of the Calvinists who worshipped here, its pulpit placed in the centre as a complete break with the Catholic past.

BLOEMGRACHT

NOORDERMARKT

MAP P.73, POCKET MAP C2

The **Noordermarkt** holds a statue of three figures bound to each other, a tribute to the bloody Jordaanoproer riot of 1934, part of a successful campaign to stop the government cutting unemployment benefit during the Depression. The square hosts some of Amsterdam's best **markets** – a household goods market on Monday mornings (9am–1pm) and the farmers' market, the **Boerenmarkt**, on Saturdays (9am–4pm).

LINDENGRACHT

MAP P.73, POCKET MAP C1

The **Lindengracht** ("Canal of Limes") lost its waterway decades ago, and is a fairly nondescript thoroughfare, though it is home to the Suyckerhofje of 1667 – easy to miss through a mall gateway at no. 149, and with a lovely enclosed garden that is typical of the Jordaan's many *hofjes*.

THE SCHEEPVAARTSBUURT AND THE WESTERDOK

MAP P.73, POCKET MAP C1

Brouwersgracht marks both the northern edge of the Jordaan and the southern boundary of the **Scheepvaartsbuurt** – the Shipping Quarter. In the eighteenth and nineteenth centuries, this district boomed from its location between the Brouwersgracht and the Westerdok, a long and slender parcel of land dredged out of the River IJ immediately to the north and equipped with docks, warehouses and shipyards. The **Westerdok** hung on to some of the marine trade until the 1960s, but today industry has to all intents and purposes disappeared and the area is busy reinventing itself, as the old warehouses are turned into apartments. The nearby **Westerpark** provides a spot of green for the locals, and the **Westergasfabriek** (Ⓦwww.westergasfabriek.nl), a former gasworks converted into a cultural zone full of design companies and restaurants; it hosts a fashion market on the first Sunday of each month. A short walk away, under the rail tracks and left down Zaanstraat, the 1921 **Het Schip** housing development is a seminal work of the Amsterdam School and can be visited on hourly tours (Ⓦwww.hetschip.nl, Tues–Sun 11am–5pm; €7.50).

Shops

ADRIAN

Prinsengracht 130. Tues–Sat noon–6pm.
MAP P.73, POCKET MAP C3

Truly a one-off, Adrian buys
fabrics from all over the world
and makes them up into shirts,
trousers and suits in fantastic
gaudy, floral designs.

BLOEMBOLLENWINKEL

Prinsengracht 112. Daily 10am–6pm. MAP P.73,
POCKET MAP C2

Charming little shop selling
packets of tulip bulbs in
season. Downstairs is a small
museum (€6) that charts the
tulip's history from the gardens
of the Ottoman Empire to
becoming Amsterdam's most
iconic flower.

COPPENHAGEN

Rozengracht 54. Mon 1–6pm, Sat 10am–5pm.
MAP P.73, POCKET MAP B3

Something of a Jordaan
institution, this shop stocks
beads and beady accessories –
including everything you'll
need to make your own
jewellery.

ENGLISH BOOKSHOP

Lauriergracht 71. Tues–Sat 11am–6pm.
MAP P.72, POCKET MAP B4

Stocks a well-chosen collection
of titles on a wide range of
subjects, in particular literature.

JORDINO

Haarlemmerdijk 25a. Mon 1–7pm, Tues–Sat
10am–7pm, Sun 1–7pm. MAP P.72, POCKET MAP D1

Fantastic handmade chocolates
and some of the best ice cream
in the city.

KITSCH KITCHEN

Rozengracht 8. Mon–Sat 10am–6pm, Sun
noon–5pm. MAP P.72, POCKET MAP C3

Crammed full of chunky
furniture and brightly coloured

BARNEY'S

bowls and other home and
kitchen stuff – you're bound to
find something you think you
need here.

OUD-HOLLANDSCH SNOEPWINKELTJE

Tweede Egelantierdwarsstraat 2. Tues–Sat
11am–6.30pm, Sun noon–5pm. MAP P.73,
POCKET MAP B2

Delicious Dutch sweets, piled
up in glass jars attracting
hordes of kids.

Coffeeshops

BARNEY'S

Haarlemmerstraat 102. Daily 7am–1am. MAP
P.73, POCKET MAP D1

This popular coffeeshop is the
most civilized place in town to
enjoy a big hit before moving
on to *Barney's Uptown* across
the road for a drink.

PARADOX

1e Bloemdwarsstraat 2. Daily 10am–8pm.
MAP P.73, POCKET MAP B3

Paradox satisfies the munchies
with outstanding natural food,
including spectacular fresh
fruit concoctions and veggie
burgers.

Cafés and tearooms

ARNOLD CORNELIS

Elandsgracht 78. Mon–Fri 8.30am–6pm, Sat 8.30am–5pm. MAP P.73, POCKET MAP B4

Confectioner and patisserie with a mouth-watering display of pastries and cakes. Take away or eat in the snug tearoom.

FESTINA LENTE

Looiersgracht 40b. Mon noon–1am, Tues–Thurs 10.30am–1/3am, Fri & Sat 10.30am–3am, Sun noon–1am. MAP P.73, POCKET MAP B4

Relaxed café-bar with armchairs to laze about on. The outside tables overlooking the canal are a suntrap in the summer.

WINKEL 43

Noordermarkt 43. Mon 7am–1am, Tues–Thurs 8am–1am, Fri 8am–3am, Sat 7am–3am, Sun 10am–1am. MAP P.73, POCKET MAP C2

Queue up along with the rest of Amsterdam for delectable mouthwatering apple-pie –it's homemade in this agreeable lunchroom-cum-restaurant.

Restaurants

BALTHAZAR'S KEUKEN

Elandsgracht 108. ☎ 020/420 2114. Wed–Fri from 6pm. MAP P.73, POCKET MAP B4

As the name suggests, this restaurant makes you feel like you accidentally stumbled into someone's kitchen. Their weekly changing three-course menu (€27.50) is very popular. Be sure to book.

CINEMA PARADISO

Westerstraat 186. ☎ 020/623 7344. Wed–Sun 6–11pm. MAP P.73, POCKET MAP C2

Slick place covering all the Italian classics with gusto. It's in a former moviehouse and very popular, so you may have to shout to be heard. Pasta and pizzas from €12.

DUENDE

Lindengracht 62 ☎ 020/420 6692. Mon–Thurs 5pm–1am, Fri & Sat 4pm–3am, Sun 4pm–1am. Kitchen until 11pm. MAP P.73, POCKET MAP C1

Busy tapas bar with a tiled interior and a warm and inviting feel. Good food, and there's also a small venue that hosts flamenco at weekends.

LA OLIVA

Egelantiersstraat 122 ☎ 020/320 4316. Daily except Tues noon–10.30pm. MAP P.73, POCKET MAP B2

This sleek Jordaan eatery specializes in *pinxtos*, the delectable Basque snacks-on-sticks that make Spanish bar-hopping such a delight.

SEMHAR

Marnixstraat 259–261 ☎ 020/638 1634. Tues–Sun 4–10pm. MAP P.73, POCKET MAP D1

A small and popular Ethiopian restaurant with an authentic menu of meat, fish and veggie dishes – all mopped up with great East African flatbread. Try the African beer too, served in a *calabash* and available in a variety of exotic flavours. Mains from around €11.

WINKEL 43

MOEDERS

Rozengracht 251 ☎ 020/626 7957.
Mon–Fri 5pm–midnight, Sat & Sun noon–midnight, kitchen till 10.30pm. MAP P.73,
POCKET MAP B3

Really cosy restaurant just across from the Singelgracht whose theme is obvious the moment you walk in – mothers, photos of whom plaster the walls. Food is engagingly homespun Dutch grub with the odd modern twist, very tasty and reasonably priced.

DE REIGER

Nieuwe Leliestraat 34 ☎ 020/624 7426.
Tues–Fri & Sun 5–10.30pm, Sat noon–10.30pm. MAP P.73, POCKET MAP C3

In the thick of the Jordaan, this is an old-style café filled with modish Amsterdammers. Dinner around €25.

TOSCANINI

Lindengracht 75 ☎ 020/623 2813. Mon–Sat 6pm–1.30am, kitchen till 10.30pm. MAP P.73,
POCKET MAP C1

Big, bustling and very authentic Italian restaurant, with great daily specials and an extensive and delicious wine list of regional Italian wines. Excellent service and a nice atmosphere.

Bars

BARNEY'S UPTOWN

Haarlemmerstraat 105. Daily 8am–1am, Fri & Sat until 3am. MAP P.73, POCKET MAP D1

Pleasant, smoker-friendly bar that's the slick night-time sister of the coffeeshop across the street (see p.76), with DJs providing a humming backdrop. The American(ish) menu has a choice of burgers, steaks and sandwiches, and they also specialize in huge breakfasts and weekend brunch.

DE BLAFFENDE VIS

Westerstraat 118. Daily 9am–1am, Fri & Sat until 3am. MAP P.73, POCKET MAP C2

Somewhat of an institution, this typical neighbourhood bar sits at the corner of the 2e Boomdwarsstraat. Nothing pretentious, but oodles of atmosphere and a well-priced bar menu.

CAFÉ CHRIS

Bloemstraat 42. Daily 3pm–1am, Fri & Sat until 2am, Sun until 9pm. MAP P.73,
POCKET MAP B3

This place is very proud of itself for being the Jordaan's (and Amsterdam's) oldest bar –it dates from 1624. The atmosphere is homely and cosy.

FINCH

Noordermarkt 5. Daily 10am–1am, Fri & Sat until 3am, lunch from noon, dinner from 6pm.
MAP P.73, POCKET MAP C1

This smart café-lounge bar situated near the Noorderkerk attracts a stylish crowd, who come here to enjoy the design-school ambience, good tunes and superb location.

FINCH

DE HEGERAAD

Noordermarkt 34. Mon–Sat 8am–midnight, Sun 11am–11pm. MAP P.73, POCKET MAP C2

Lovingly maintained brown café with a loyal clientele. The back room is the perfect place to relax with a hot chocolate.

DE KAT IN DE WIJNGAERT

Lindengracht 160. Sun–Thurs 10am–1am, Fri 10am–3am, Sat 9am–3am MAP P.73, POCKET MAP C1

With the enticing name "The Cat in the Vineyard", this small bar is the epitome of the Jordaan local – and quiet enough for conversation.

NOL

Westerstraat 109. Daily except Tues 9pm–3am. MAP P.73, POCKET MAP C2

Raucous and jolly Jordaan singing bar. This luridly lit dive closes late, especially at weekends, when the back-slapping joviality and drunken sing-alongs keep you rooted until the small hours.

PROUST

Noordermarkt 4. Mon 9am–1am, Tues–Thurs noon–1am, Fri noon–3am, Sat 9.30am–3am, Sun noon–1am. MAP P.73, POCKET MAP C1

Trendy bar (check out the giant "gun" chandelier) with a laidback Jordaan atmosphere, attracting students and young urban professionals. Reasonably priced bar menu (burgers from €11) and drinks.

'T SMALLE

Egelantiersgracht 12. Wed–Sun 6–11pm. MAP P.73, POCKET MAP C2

Candle-lit and comfortable, this is one of Amsterdam's oldest cafés: it opened in 1786 as a tasting house for the (long-gone) gin distillery next door. Its "floating" terrace is a perfect spot in summer – arrive early to nab a table.

DE TUIN

CAFÉ THIJSSEN

Brouwersgracht 107. Mon–Thurs 8am–1am, Fri 8am–3am, Sat 7.30am–3am, Sun 9am–1am. MAP P.73, POCKET MAP C1

An old-time favourite with neighbourhood locals. Nothing fancy, but perfect to linger over coffee or fresh mint tea with a magazine. Does a decent range of soups and sandwiches.

DE TUIN

2e Tuindwarsstraat 13. Daily 10am–1am, Fri & Sat until 3am, Sun from 11am. MAP P.73, POCKET MAP C2

The Jordaan has some marvellously unpretentious bars, and this is one of the best: unkempt and always filled with locals.

Music venues

MALOE MELO

Lijnbaansgracht 163 ☎ 020/420 4592, ⓦ www.maloemelo.com. MAP P.73, POCKET MAP B4

Dark, low-ceilinged bar, with a small back room featuring local blues acts. Jam sessions take place Sunday to Thursday.

The Old Jewish Quarter and Eastern docklands

The narrow slice of land sandwiched between the curve of the River Amstel, Oudeschans and the Nieuwe Herengracht was the home of Amsterdam's Jews from the sixteenth century up until World War II. By the 1920s, this Old Jewish Quarter, or Jodenhoek ("Jews' Corner"), was crowded with tenement buildings and smoking factories, its main streets holding scores of open-air stalls selling everything from pickled herrings to pots and pans. The war put paid to all this. In 1945 it lay derelict, and neither has postwar redevelopment treated it kindly; new building has robbed the district of much of its character. But persevere: among the cars and concrete around Waterlooplein and
Mr Visserplein are several moving reminders of the Jewish community that perished in the war, while the neighbouring residential area of Plantagebuurt is home to the Artis Zoo and the excellent Verzetsmuseum (Dutch Resistance Museum). From here it's a short hop north to Oosterdok, where pride of place goes to the Nederlands –Scheepvaartmuseum (Maritime Museum), housed in what was once the arsenal of the Dutch navy.

THE REMBRANDTHUIS

Jodenbreestraat 4 ☏ 020/520 0400,
ⓦ www.rembrandthuis.nl. Daily 10am–5pm.
€10. MAP PP.82–83, POCKET MAP E4

St Antoniesbreestraat runs into Jodenbreestraat, the "Broad Street of the Jews", which was once the main centre of Jewish activity. This ancient thoroughfare is short on charm, but it is home to the **Rembrandthuis**, whose intricate facade is decorated with pretty wooden shutters. Rembrandt bought this house at the height of his fame and popularity, living here for over twenty years and spending a fortune on furnishings – an expense that ultimately contributed to his bankruptcy. An inventory made at the time details the huge collection of paintings, sculptures and art treasures he'd amassed, almost all of which was auctioned off after he was declared insolvent and forced to move to a more modest house in the Jordaan in 1658.

The city council bought the Jodenbreestraat house in 1907 and has revamped the premises on several occasions, most recently in 1999. A visit begins in the modern building next door, but you're soon into the string of period rooms that have been returned to something like their appearance when Rembrandt lived here, with the original inventory as a guide. The period furniture is enjoyable enough, especially the box-beds, and the great man's studio is surprisingly large and well-lit, but there are no Rembrandt paintings on display except when there are special exhibitions (for which expect to pay extra). However, the museum possesses an extensive collection of Rembrandt's etchings and prints as well as several of the original copper plates on which he worked, and these are on display when temporary exhibitions allow. To see more of Rembrandt's paintings, head for the Rijksmuseum (see p.95).

GASSAN DIAMONDS

Nieuwe Uilenburgerstraat 173 ☏ 020/622 5333, ⓦ www.gassan.com. Frequent 1hr guided tours daily 9am–5pm. Free; no advance booking required. MAP PP.82–83, POCKET MAP F4

Gassan Diamonds occupies a large and imposing brick building dating from 1897. Before World War II, many local Jews worked as diamond cutters and polishers, but there's little sign of the industry hereabouts today, this factory being the main exception. Tours include a visit to the cutting and polishing areas, as well a gambol round Gassan's diamond jewellery showroom.

THE STADHUIS EN MUZIEKTHEATER

Muziektheater box office ☎ 020/625 5455, Ⓦ www.het-muziektheater.nl. MAP PP.82–83, POCKET MAP E5

Jodenbreestraat runs parallel to the **Stadhuis en Muziektheater**, a sprawling and distinctly underwhelming modern complex dating from the 1980s and incorporating the city hall and a large auditorium. The Muziektheater offers a varied programme of theatre, dance and ballet as well as opera from the country's first-rate Netherlands Opera (De Nederlandse Opera; Ⓦ www.dno.nl), but tickets go very quickly. One of the city's abiding ironies is that the title of the protest campaign aiming to prevent the development in the 1980s – "Stopera" – has passed into common usage to describe the finished item. Inside, amid all the architectural mediocrity, there are a couple of minor attractions, beginning with the glass columns in the public passageway towards the rear of the complex. These give a salutary lesson on the fragility of the Netherlands: two columns contain water indicating the sea levels in the Dutch towns of Vlissingen and IJmuiden (below knee height), while another records the levels experienced during the 1953 flood disaster (way above head height). At their base, a concrete pile shows what is known as "Normal Amsterdam Level" (NAP), originally calculated in 1684 as the average water level in the river IJ and still the basis for measuring altitude above sea level across Europe.

Old Jewish Quarter & Eastern docklands

CAFÉS	
Blijburg aan Zee	3
Dantzig	11
De Hortus	13
Kadijk	7
Staalmeesters	12

RESTAURANTS	
Eénvistwéévis	5
Fifteen	1
Greetje	4
Kilimanjaro	6
Koffiehuis van de Volksbond	9

BARS	
Brouwerij 't IJ	14
De Druif	8
KHL Koffiehuis	2
De Sluyswacht	10

CLUBS & MUSIC VENUES	
Bimhuis	2
Muziekgebouw	1
Pakhuis Wilhelmina	3
Panama	4

ACCOMMODATION	
Adolesce	2
Lloyd Hotel	1

SHOP	
Gall & Gall	1

WATERLOOPLEIN

MAP PP.82–83, POCKET MAP E5–F5

The indeterminate modernity of the Stadhuis complex dominates **Waterlooplein**, a rectangular parcel of land that was originally swampy marsh. This was the site of the first Jewish Quarter, but by the late nineteenth century it had become an insanitary slum. The slums were cleared in the 1880s and thereafter the open spaces of the Waterlooplein hosted the largest and liveliest market in the city, the place where Jews and Gentiles met to trade. In the war, the Germans used the square to round up their victims, but despite these ugly connotations the Waterlooplein was revived in the 1950s as the site of the city's main **flea market** (Mon–Sat 9am–5pm) and remains so to this day. It's

nowhere near as large as it once was, but nonetheless it's still the final resting place of many a pair of yellow corduroy flares and has some wonderful antique and junk stalls to root through. If you're after a bargain, head there early, as it's very popular with tourists.

Nearby, at the very tip of Waterlooplein, where the River Amstel meets the Zwanenburgwal canal, there is a sombre **memorial** – a black stone tribute to the dead of the Jewish resistance. The inscription from Jeremiah translates, "If my eyes were a well of tears, I would cry day and night for the fallen fighters of my beloved people." Metres away, a second sculpture honours philosopher and theologian **Baruch Spinoza** who was born nearby in 1632.

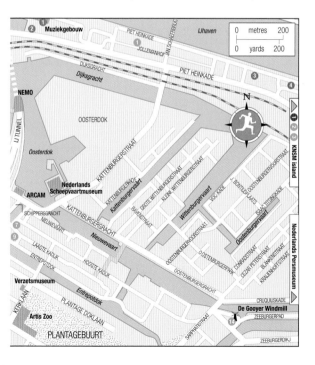

THE ESNOGA

MR VISSERPLEIN

MAP PP.82–83, POCKET MAP F4

Just behind the Muziek-theater, on the corner of **Mr Visserplein**, is the **Mozes en Aaron Kerk**, a rather glum Neoclassical structure built on the site of a clandestine Catholic church in the 1840s. The square itself, a busy junction for traffic speeding towards the IJ tunnel, takes its name from Mr Visser, President of the Supreme Court of the Netherlands in 1939. He was dismissed the following year when the Germans occupied the country, and became an active member of the Jewish resistance, working for the illegal underground newspaper *Het Parool* ("The Password") and refusing to wear the yellow Star of David. He died in 1942, a few days after publicly – and famously – denouncing all forms of collaboration.

THE ESNOGA

Mr Visserplein ☎ 020/531 0380, ⓦ www. esnoga.com. April–Oct Sun–Fri 10am–4pm; Nov–March Sun–Thurs 10am–4pm & Fri 10am–2pm; closed Yom Kippur. €12. MAP PP.82–83, POCKET MAP F5

The brown and bulky brickwork of the **Esnoga** or Portuguese synagogue was completed in 1675 for the city's Sephardic community. One of Amsterdam's most imposing buildings, it has been barely altered since its construction, its lofty interior following the Sephardic tradition in having the *Hechal* (the Ark of the Covenant) and *tebah* (from where services are led) at opposite ends. Also traditional is the seating, with two sets of wooden benches (for the men) facing each other across the central aisle – the women have separate galleries up above. A set of superb brass chandeliers holds the candles that remain the only source of artificial light. When it was completed, the synagogue was one of the largest in the world, its congregation almost certainly the richest; today, the Sephardic community has dwindled to just a few families. In one of the outhouses, a video sheds light on the history of the synagogue and Amsterdam's Sephardim. The mystery is why the Nazis left the building alone – no one knows for sure, but it seems likely that they intended to turn it into a museum once all the Jews had been polished off.

TUNFUN

Mr Visserplein 7 📞 020/689 4300, 🌐 www
.tunfun.nl. Daily 10am–6pm. Children 1–12
€8.50, free for adults and under-1s. MAP
PP.82–83, POCKET MAP F5

This large **indoor playground**
near the Portuguese synagogue
has lots of equipment to
clamber into, under and over,
and a host of kids' activities
and workshops including
football, gymnastics, films and
trampolining. Children must
be accompanied by an adult,
and there's a café to sit in if you
feel you've already been in one
ball park too many.

JONAS DANIEL MEIJERPLEIN

MAP PP.82–83, POCKET MAP F5

Jonas Daniel Meijerplein was
where, in February 1941,
around 400 Jewish men were
loaded onto trucks and taken to
their deaths at Mauthausen
concentration camp, in reprisal
for the killing of a Dutch Nazi
during a street fight. The arrests
sparked off the February Strike,
a general strike in protest
against the Germans' treatment
of the Jews. It was organized by
the outlawed Communist Party
and spearheaded by
Amsterdam's transport workers
and dockers in a rare
demonstration of solidarity
with the Jews. The strike was
quickly suppressed, but is still
commemorated by an annual
wreath-laying ceremony on
February 25, as well as by Mari
Andriessen's statue *The
Dokwerker* (Dockworker)
standing on the square.

JOODS HISTORISCH MUSEUM

Nieuwe Amstelstraat 1 📞 020/531 0310,
🌐 www.jhm.nl. Daily 11am–5pm; closed Yom
Kippur. €12. MAP PP.82–83, POCKET MAP F5

The **Joods Historisch Museum**
(Jewish Historical Museum) is
cleverly shoehorned into four
adjacent Ashkenazi synagogues
that date from the late
seventeenth century. For years
after World War II these
buildings lay abandoned, but
they were finally refurbished –
and connected by walkways – in
the 1980s, to accommodate a
Jewish exhibition centre.

The first major display area,
just beyond the reception desk
on the ground floor of the
Nieuwe Synagoge, features
temporary exhibitions on
Jewish life and culture with
vintage photographs to the fore.
Upstairs is a history of Dutch
Jewry from 1900 to the present.
Inevitably, the emphasis is on
the calamity that befell them
during the German occupation
of World War II, but there is
also a biting display on the
indifferent/hostile reaction of
many Dutch men and women
to liberated Jews in 1945.
Moving on, the ground floor of
the adjacent **Grote Synagoge**
holds an engaging display on
Jewish culture. There is a fine
collection of religious silverware
here, plus all manner of antique
artefacts illustrating religious
customs and practices. The
gallery up above holds a finely
judged social history of the
country's Jewish population
from 1600 to 1900.

JOODS HISTORISCH MUSEUM

HERMITAGE AMSTERDAM

Amstel 51 ☎ 020/530 7488, ⓦ www
.hermitage.nl. Daily 10am–5pm. €15. MAP
PP.82–83, POCKET MAP F5

Backing onto the River Amstel, the stern-looking **Amstelhof** started out as a *hofje*, or almshouse for the care of elderly women, built in the 1680s on behalf of the Dutch Reformed Church. In time, it grew to fill most of the land between Nieuwe Herengracht and Nieuwe Keizersgracht, becoming a fully-fledged hospital in the process, but in the 1980s it became clear that its medical facilities were out of date and it went up for sale. Much municipal huffing and puffing ensued until someone had a brainwave – the idea being to convert it into a museum, **Hermitage Amsterdam**, for the display of items loaned from the Hermitage in St Petersburg. It was a very ambitious scheme, with the historic exterior preserved and a light, modern interior created inside. Completed in 2009, its substantial number of galleries now display prime pieces from the Hermitage. Exhibitions, which usually last about five months, have included "Nicholas & Alexandra" and "Impressionism: Sensation & Inspiration".

THE PLANTAGEBUURT

MAP PP.82–83, POCKET MAP G5–H5

Developed in the middle of the nineteenth century, the **Plantagebuurt**, with its comfortable streets spreading to either side of the Plantage Middenlaan boulevard, was built as part of a concerted attempt to provide good-quality housing for the city's expanding middle classes. Although it was never as fashionable as the older residential parts of the Grachtengordel (see p.52–71), the new district did contain elegant villas and spacious terraces, making it a first suburban port of call for many aspiring Jews. Nowadays, the Plantagebuurt is still one of the more prosperous parts of the city, in a modest sort of way, and boasts two especially enjoyable attractions – the Hortus Botanicus botanical gardens and the Verzetsmuseum (Dutch Resistance Museum).

HORTUS BOTANICUS

Plantage Middenlaan 2a ☎ 020/625 9021,
ⓦ www.dehortus.nl. Daily 10am–5pm. €7.50.
MAP PP.82–83, POCKET MAP F5–G4

Amsterdam's lush **Hortus Botanicus** were founded in 1682 as medicinal gardens for the use of the city's physicians and apothecaries. Thereafter, many of the city's merchants made a point of bringing back exotic species from the East, the result being the 6000-odd plant species exhibited today. The gardens are divided into several distinct sections, each clearly labelled and its location pinpointed by a map available at the entrance kiosk.

Most of the outdoor sections are covered by plants, trees and shrubs from the temperate and Arctic zones. There's also a three-climates glasshouse, where the plants are arranged according to their geographical origins, a capacious palm house, an orchid nursery and a butterfly house. It's all very low-key – and none the worse for that – and the gardens make a relaxing break on any tour of central Amsterdam, especially as the café, in the old orangery, serves up tasty sandwiches, coffee and cakes (see p.91).

HORTUS BOTANICUS

WERTHEIMPARK

MAP PP.82–83, POCKET MAP G4

The pocket-sized **Wertheimpark**, across the road from the Hortus Botanicus, is home to the Auschwitz Monument, a simple affair with symbolically broken mirrors and an inscription that reads *Nooit meer Auschwitz* ("Auschwitz – Never Again"). It was designed by the late Dutch writer Jan Wolkers.

DE HOLLANDSCHE SCHOUWBURG

Plantage Middenlaan 24 ☏ 020/531 0340 ⊛ www.hollandscheschouwburg.nl. Daily 11am–4pm; closed Yom Kippur. Free. MAP PP.82–83, POCKET MAP G5

Another sad relic of the war, **De Hollandsche Schouwburg** was once a thriving Jewish theatre, but the Nazis turned it into the main assembly point for Amsterdam Jews prior to their deportation. Inside, there was no daylight and families were interned in conditions that foreshadowed those of the camps they would soon be taken to. The building has been refurbished to house a small exhibition on the plight of the city's Jews, but the old auditorium out at the back has been left as an empty, roofless shell. A memorial column of basalt on a Star of David base stands where the stage once was, an intensely mournful monument to suffering of unfathomable proportions.

ARTIS ZOO

Plantage Kerklaan 38–40 ☏ 020/523 3481, ⊛ www.artis.nl. Daily: April–Oct 9am–6pm; Nov–March 9am–5pm; June–Aug Sat until dusk. €19; 3- to 9-year-olds €15.50. MAP PP.82–83, POCKET MAP G5

Opened in 1838, **Artis Zoo** is the oldest zoo in the Netherlands and one of the city's top tourist attractions, though thankfully its layout and refreshing lack of bars and cages mean that it never feels overcrowded. Highlights include an African savanna environment, a seventy-metre-long aviary, aquaria and a South American zone with llamas and the world's largest rodent, the capybara. Feeding times – always popular – include 11am for the birds of prey; 11.30am and 3.45pm seals and sea lions; 2pm pelicans; 12.30pm crocodiles (Sun only); 3pm lions and tigers (not Thurs); and 3.30pm penguins. In addition, the on-site Planetarium has five or six shows daily, all in Dutch, though you can pick up a leaflet with an English translation from the desk.

VERZETSMUSEUM

Plantage Kerklaan 61 ☎ 020/620 2535,
ⓦ www.verzetsmuseum.org, Mon, Sat & Sun
11am–5pm. Tues–Fri 10am–5pm, €8. MAP
PP.82–83, POCKET MAP G5

The excellent **Verzetsmuseum**
(Dutch Resistance Museum)
outlines the development of the
Dutch Resistance from the
German invasion of the
Netherlands in May 1940 to the
country's liberation in 1945.
The main themes of the
occupation are dealt with
honestly, noting the fine
balance between cooperation
and collaboration, while
smaller displays focus on
aspects such as the protest
against the rounding-up of
Amsterdam's Jews in 1941 and
the so-called Milk Strike of
1943. There are fascinating old
photographs and a host of
original artefacts including
examples of illegal newsletters
and, chillingly, signed German
death warrants. The museum
also has dozens of little metal
sheets providing biographical
sketches of the members of the
Resistance.

THE OOSTERDOK

MAP PP.82–83, POCKET MAP H3–H4

Just to the north of the
Plantagebuurt lies the
Oosterdok, whose network of
artificial islands was dredged
out of the River IJ to increase
Amsterdam's shipping facilities
in the seventeenth century. By
the 1980s, this mosaic of docks,
jetties and islands had become
something of a post-industrial
eyesore, but since then an
ambitious redevelopment
programme has turned things
around. Easily the most
agreeable way of reaching the
Oosterdok is via the footbridge
at the north end of Plantage
Kerklaan – and metres from
the Verzetsmuseum – which
leads onto Entrepotdok.

ENTREPOTDOK

MAP PP.82–83, POCKET MAP G4–G5

Over the footbridge at the end
of Plantage Kerklaan lies one
of the more interesting of the
Oosterdok islands, a slender
rectangle whose southern
quayside, **Entrepotdok**, is
lined by a long series of
nineteenth-century gabled
warehouses that were once
part of the largest warehouse
complex in continental
Europe. Each warehouse
sports the name of a town or
island; goods for onward
transportation were stored in
the appropriate warehouse
until there were enough to fill
a boat or barge. The

warehouses have been converted into offices and apartments, a fate that must surely befall the buildings of the central East India Company compound, at the west end of Entrepotdok on Kadijksplein.

NEDERLANDS SCHEEPVAARTMUSEUM

Kattenburgerplein ☎ 020/523 2222, ⓦ www .hetscheepvaartmuseum.nl. Daily 9am–5pm. €15.

One of the city's most popular attractions, the **Nederlands Scheepvaartmuseum** (Netherlands Maritime Museum) occupies the old arsenal of the Dutch navy, a vast sandstone structure built on the Oosterdok in the seventeenth century. Visitors get their bearings in the central **courtyard** from where you can enter any one of three display areas – labelled "West", "Noord" and "Oost". Of the three, the **West** displays are the most child-orientated, the **Oost** the most substantial, including garish ships' figureheads, examples of early atlases, globes and navigational equipment. There are many nautical paintings in this section too, some devoted to the achievements of Dutch trading ships, others showing heavy seas and shipwrecks and yet more celebrating the successes of the Dutch navy, the most powerful fleet in the world from the 1650s to the 1680s. Willem van de Velde II (1633–1707) was the most successful of the Dutch marine painters of the period and there's a good sample of his work here.

The "**Noord**" section features a couple of short nautical films and also gives access to the 78-metre De Amsterdam, a full-scale replica of an East Indiaman merchant ship. The original vessel first set sail in 1748, but came to an ignominious end, getting stuck on the English coast near Hastings. Visitors can wander the ship's decks and galleys, storerooms and gun bays at their leisure.

NEMO

Oosterdok ☎ 020/531 3233, ⓦ www.e-nemo.nl. Tues–Sun 10am–5pm, plus Mon 10am–5pm during school hols and June–Aug. €13.50. MAP PP.82–83, POCKET MAP G3

Hard to miss in the eastern docklands is the massive elevated hood that rears up above the entrance to the IJ tunnel. A good part of this is occupied by the lavish **NEMO** centre, a (pre-teenage) kids' attraction par excellence, with all sorts of interactive science and technological exhibits spread over six floors and set out under several broad themes.

THE MUZIEKGEBOUW

Piet Heinkade 1 ☎ 020/788 2000. No fixed
opening times – open for performances.
MAP PP.82–83, POCKET MAP G2

One of the Eastern dockland's
prime buildings, the
Muziekgebouw is a high-spec,
multipurpose music
auditorium overlooking the
River IJ. It encompasses two
medium-sized concert halls,
a café and a bar. It also has
state-of-the-art acoustics,
and has given real impetus to
the redevelopment going on
along the IJ. As well as some
contemporary music, it has a
good programme of opera and
orchestral music which brings a
rather highbrow crowd to this
part of town – and it's worth a
visit for the building alone.

ZEEBURG

MAP PP.82–83, POCKET MAP A3

On the northeast edge of the
city centre, **Zeeburg** – basically
the old docklands between the
Muziekgebouw and **KNSM
Island** – has become one of the
city's most up-and-coming
districts. Actually a series of
artificial islands and peninsulas
connected by bridges, the
docks here date back to the end
of the nineteenth century. By
the early 1990s, the area was
virtually derelict so the city
council began a massive
renovation, which has been
going on for the past fifteen
years or so. As a result, this is
the fastest-developing part of
Amsterdam, with a mixture of
renovated dockside structures
and new landmark buildings
that give it a modern (and very
watery) feel that's markedly
different from the city centre –
despite beginning just a
ten-minute walk from Centraal
Station. Explore the area by
bike, especially as distances are,
at least in Amsterdam terms,
comparatively large – from the
Muziekgebouw to the east end
of KNSM Island is about 4km.

Alternatively, there are two
useful transport connections
from Centraal Station: tram
#26 to Sporenburg island via
Piet Heinkade and bus #42 to
Java Island and KNSM Island.

NEDERLANDS PERSMUSEUM

Zeeburgerkade 10. ☎ 020/692 8810. ⓦ www
.persmuseum.nl. Tues–Fri 10am–5pm & Sun
noon–5pm. €4.50. MAP PP.82–83.

From the west end of Borneo
island to the south of KNSM
Island, C van Eesterenlaan
slices south across a wide strip
of water, the old Entrepothaven,
bound for Zeeburgerkade,
which is home to the
Nederlands Persmuseum. The
museum has a mildly
interesting series of displays on
the leading Dutch
newspapermen of yesteryear,
beginning with Abraham
Casteleyn, who first published a
combined business and political
newssheet in the 1650s.

Of more immediate interest
perhaps are the cartoons, often
vitriolic attacks on those in
power both in the Netherlands
and elsewhere; for instance,
the last premier – Jan Peter
Balkenende – is often
mockingly portrayed as Harry
Potter (he looks like him).

THE MUZIEKGEBOUW

Shops

GALL & GALL

Jodenbreestraat 23. Mon–Wed 9am–9pm, Thurs–Sat 9am–10pm, Sun 11am–8pm. MAP PP.82–83, POCKET MAP F4

Has an outstanding range of Dutch *jenevers* (gins) and flavoured spirits as well as a good selection of imported wines. Part of a popular chain.

Cafés

BLIJBURG AAN ZEE

Muiderlaan 1001. Wed–Sun noon–10pm. MAP PP.82–83, POCKET MAP H3

Amsterdam's own city beach might be something of a disappointment, but *Blijburg* is very much happening with DJs in summer and live music in winter. Last stop of tram #26 from Centraal Station.

DANTZIG

Zwanenburgwal 15. Daily 9am–10pm, Sat & Sun from 10am. MAP PP.82–83, POCKET MAP E4

Easy-going grand café, right next to the Muziektheater. Comfortable chairs, friendly service and a low-key, chic atmosphere. The kitchen is open all day, except for a brief break 5–6pm.

DE HORTUS

Plantage Middenlaan 2a. Daily 10am–4.30pm. MAP PP.82–83, POCKET MAP F5

The café in the orangery of the Hortus Botanicus (see p.86) serves tasty sandwiches and rolls plus the best blueberry cheesecake on Earth. You do, however, have to pay to get into the gardens to get to the café.

KADIJK

Kadijksplein 5. Tues–Sun noon–10pm, Mon 4–10pm. MAP PP.82–83, POCKET MAP G4

Tiny place which – contrary to what the homely interior with

DE HORTUS

Delft blue crockery might suggest – has an excellent Indonesian inspired menu. Tasty chicken or beef *saté* goes for €12.50. For dessert try the traditional Indonesian *spekkoek* (spiced cake) served with coffee.

STAALMEESTERS

Kloveniersburgwal 127. Daily 10am–10.30pm. MAP PP.82–83, POCKET MAP E4

Cosy if cramped café, with wooden tables and a big replica of Rembrandt's *Staalmeesters* on the wall. Breakfast until 4.30pm for the genuine night crawler and a small selection of cocktails.

Restaurants

ÉÉNVISTWÉÉVIS

Schippersgracht 6 ☎ 020/623 2894. Tues–Sat 6–10pm. MAP PP.82–83, POCKET MAP G4

A great fish restaurant serving an interesting selection of seafood, such as seabass with rosemary and thyme complemented by well-chosen wines. Mains around €20.

FIFTEEN

Jollemanshof 9 ☎ 020/509 5015. Mon–Sat
noon–3pm & 5.30pm–1am, Sun dinner only,
kitchen till 10pm. MAP PP.82–83, POCKET MAP H2

The Amsterdam branch of
Jamie Oliver's successful
restaurant formula, which
annually gives a bunch of
youngsters the chance to work
in a top-notch kitchen. The
food sticks to the Oliver
template with a menu described
as "modern Mediterranean with
Italian influences" – expect lots
of fresh olives and buffalo
mozzarella to start followed by
imaginative pasta (truffle and
egg yolk ravioli – €12) and
risotto dishes, plus daily
changing meat and fish mains
(from €21.50). There's also a
less formal trattoria and lounge.

GREETJE

Peperstraat 23 ☎ 020/779 7450. Daily
6–10.30pm. MAP PP.82–83, POCKET MAP F4

A cosy, busy restaurant that
serves up Dutch staples with a
modern twist. A changing
menu (mains around €25)
reflects the seasons and the
favourite dishes of the owner's
mother – a native of the
southern Netherlands. Superb
home-cooking in a great
atmosphere.

GREETJE

KILIMANJARO

Rapenburgerplein 6 ☎ 020/622 3485. Tues–
Sun 5–10pm. MAP PP.82–83, POCKET MAP G4

African restaurant in a largely
forgotten part of town, serving
West African antelope goulash,
Moroccan *tajine* and crocodile
steak. Vegetarian options
available. Small, moderately
priced and super-friendly.

KOFFIEHUIS VAN DE VOLKSBOND

Kadijksplein 4 ☎ 020/622 1209. Daily
6–10pm. MAP PP.82–83, POCKET MAP G4

Once a dockworkers' café, this
is now a popular Oosterdok
café-restaurant. The eclectic
menu packs in everything from
Thai fishcake starters (€7.75) to
Moroccan style lamb and
Cajun gumbo mains (€16.50).

Bars

BROUWERIJ 'T IJ

De Gooyer windmill, Funenkade 7. Daily
3–8pm. MAP PP.82–83, POCKET MAP H5

Well-established if somewhat
frugal bar and mini-brewery in
the old public baths adjoining
the De Gooyer windmill.
Serves up an excellent range of
beers and ales, from the
thunderously strong Columbus
amber ale (9%) to the creamier,
more soothing Natte (6.5%).

DE DRUIF

Rapenburgerplein 83. Daily 3pm–1am, Fri &
Sat until 2am. MAP PP.82–83, POCKET MAP G4

"The Grape" is one of the city's
oldest bars (dating from 1631),
and certainly one of its more
beguiling. A popular
neighbourhood joint, it pulls in
an easy-going crowd.

KHL KOFFIEHUIS

Oostelijke Handelskade 44 ☎ 020/779 1575,
⊛ www.khl.nl. Tues–Thurs 11am–1am, Fri
11am–2am, Sat noon–3am, Sun noon–1am.
MAP PP.82–83, POCKET MAP H3

Old-fashioned coffeehouse (not to be confused with coffeeshop) with wooden panelling and heavy red curtains, located in a 1917 state monument. Small but varied menu (try the signature KHL burger – €16) and live music in the backroom on Saturday and Sunday.

DE SLUYSWACHT

Jodenbreestraat 1. Mon–Sat 11.30am–1am, Fri & Sat until 3am, Sun 11.30am–7pm. MAP PP.82–83, POCKET MAP E4

This pleasant little bar occupies an old and now solitary gabled house that stands sentry by the lock gates opposite the Rembrandthuis. A smashing spot to nurse a beer on a warm summer's night, gazing down the canal towards the Montelbaanstoren.

Clubs and music venues

BIMHUIS

Piet Heinkade 3 ☎ 020/788 2188, ⓦ www.bimhuis.nl. MAP PP.82–83, POCKET MAP G2

The city's premier jazz and improvised music venue is located right next the Muziekgebouw, beside the River IJ to the east of Centraal Station. The Bimhuis showcases gigs from Dutch and international artists throughout the week, as well as jam sessions and workshops. There's also a bar and restaurant for concert-goers with pleasant views over the river.

MUZIEKGEBOUW

Piet Heinkade 1 ☎ 020/788 2000, ⓦ www.muziekgebouw.nl. MAP PP.82–83, POCKET MAP G2

Located in a modern glass building overlooking the river, the Muziekgebouw showcases everything from classical

PANAMA

through to jazz and rock, and has studios, rehearsal space and convention facilities.

PAKHUIS WILHELMINA

Veemkade 576 ☎ 020/419 3368, ⓦ www.cafépakhuiswilhelmina.nl. MAP PP.82–83, POCKET MAP H3

Tucked away in an old warehouse, this underground venue hosts everything from jazz to pop, funk, punk and folk, with live gigs and DJs from Wednesday to Sunday. Try not to miss the "hardrock karaoke" night (€5) where you can belt out a rock anthem accompanied by a live band.

PANAMA

Oostelijke Handelskade 4 ☎ 020/311 8686, ⓦ www.panama.nl. MAP PP.82–83, POCKET MAP H3

All-in-one restaurant, bar and nightclub located in the former power plant located right on the river IJ. Many live performances as well as internationally renowned DJs on weekends. One of the coolest spots in the city, *Panama* has played a leading role in spicing up the Eastern docks.

The Museum Quarter and the Vondelpark

During the nineteenth century, Amsterdam grew beyond its restraining canals, gobbling up the surrounding countryside with a slew of new, mostly residential suburbs. Museumplein once served as an introduction to these new developments, a large triangular open space surrounded by the cream of the city's museums. The largest is the Rijksmuseum, which occupies a huge late nineteenth-century edifice overlooking the Singelgracht and possesses an exceptional collection of art and applied art. Close by, the more modern Van Gogh Museum boasts the finest assortment of Van Gogh paintings in the world, while the adjacent Stedelijk Museum boasts an outstanding collection of modern art, finally back on show after a multi-million euro renovation. Out on this side of the city also is the Vondelpark, Amsterdam's largest and most attractive green space, whose gently landscaped rectangle of lawns and paths, lakes and streams provides the perfect place for a lazy picnic between museums. The leafy streets around the park, such as PC Hooftstraat, also provide some of the most upmarket shopping in Amsterdam.

MUSEUMPLEIN

MAP P.96, POCKET MAP C7

Extending south from Stadhouderskade to Van Baerlestraat, **Museumplein**'s wide lawns and gravelled spaces are used for a variety of outdoor activities, from visiting circuses to political demonstrations. There's a **war memorial** here too – it's the group of slim steel blocks about three-quarters of the way down the Museumplein on the left-hand side. It commemorates the women of the wartime concentration camps, particularly those who died at Ravensbruck.

WAR MEMORIAL, MUSEUMPLEIN

THE RIJKSMUSEUM

THE RIJKSMUSEUM

Entrance to the Philips Wing of the Rijksmuseum is on Jan Luijkenstraat ☎ 020/674 7000, ⊛ www.rijksmuseum.nl. Daily 9am–6pm. €14. MAP P.96, POCKET MAP C6

The **Rijksmuseum** is without question the country's foremost museum, with one of the world's most comprehensive collections of seventeenth-century Dutch paintings, including twenty or so of **Rembrandt**'s works, plus a healthy sample of canvases by Steen, Hals, Vermeer and their leading contemporaries. The museum also owns an extravagant collection of paintings from every other pre-twentieth-century period of Dutch art and has a vast hoard of applied art and sculpture. Much of the museum has been closed for a decade during a tortuous €375m **renovation project**, though this is set to end in late 2013. In the interim, the museum's Philips Wing has remained open with a smallish but eclectic "Masterpieces" exhibition devoted to the paintings of Amsterdam's Golden Age. Bear in mind, though, that queues can still be long, especially in summer and at weekends, so try to book online ahead of time.

Even if you do have to queue, it's still worth the wait, as the selection on display is superb. There are paintings by Rembrandt's pupils – Ferdinand Bol, Gerard Dou and Gabriel Metsu; several wonderful canvases by Frans Hals, such as his scatological *Merry Drinker*; the cool interiors of Vermeer, Gerard ter Borch and Pieter de Hooch; soft, tonal river scenes by the Haarlem artist Salomon van Ruysdael and by Albert Cuyp; the cool church interiors of Pieter Saenredam; and the popular carousing peasants of Jan Steen. However, it's the Rembrandts that steal the show, especially *The Night Watch* of 1642 – perhaps the most famous and probably the most valuable of all the artist's pictures – plus other key works, like a late *Self-Portrait*, a touching depiction of his cowled son, *Titus*, the arresting *Staalmeesters* and *The Jewish Bride*, one of his very last pictures, finished in 1667.

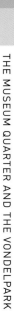

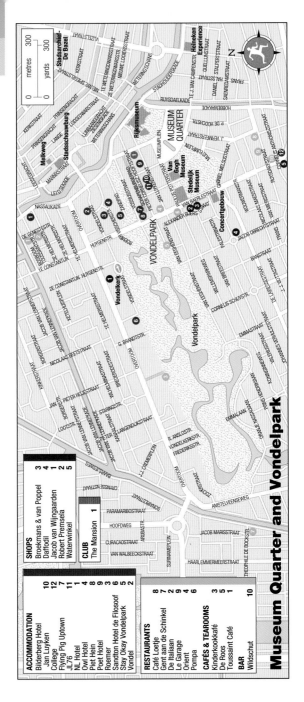

Museum Quarter and Vondelpark

ACCOMMODATION

Bilderberg Hotel	10
Jan Luyken	12
College	7
Flying Pig Uptown	11
JL76	1
NL Hotel	4
Owl Hotel	8
Piet Hein	9
Poet Hotel	3
Roemer	6
Sandton Hotel de Filosoof	5
Stay Okay Vondelpark	2

RESTAURANTS

Café Loetje	8
Gent aan de Schinkel	7
De Italiaan	9
Le Garage	4
Orient	6
Pompa	6

CAFÉS & TEAROOMS

Kinderkookkafé	3
De Roos	5
Toussaint Café	1

BAR

Wildschut	10

SHOPS

Broekmans & van Poppel	3
Daffodil	4
Jacob van Wijngaarden	1
Robert Premsela	2
Waterwinkel	5

CLUB

The Mansion	1

THE VAN GOGH MUSEUM

Paulus Potterstraat 7 ☎ 020/570 5200, ⓦ www.vangoghmuseum.nl. Daily 10am–6pm, Fri until 10pm. €14, under 17 free. MAP P.96, POCKET MAP B7

The **Van Gogh Museum**, comprising a fabulous collection of the artist's (1853–90) work, is one of Amsterdam's top attractions. The museum occupies two modern buildings, with the kernel of the collection housed in an angular building at the front designed by a leading light of the De Stijl movement, Gerrit Rietveld, and opened to the public in 1973. Beautifully presented, this part of the museum provides an introduction to the man and his art based on paintings that were mostly inherited from Vincent's art-dealer brother Theo.

All of Van Gogh's key paintings are featured on the **first floor**, displayed chronologically, starting with the dark, sombre works of the early years like *The Potato Eaters* and finishing up with the asylum years at St Rémy and the final, tortured paintings done at Auvers, where Van Gogh lodged for the last three months of his life. It was at Auvers that he painted the frantic *Wheatfield with Crows* and the disturbing *Tree Roots*.

It was a few weeks after completing these last paintings that Van Gogh shot and fatally wounded himself.

The two floors above provide back-up to the main collection. The **second floor** has a study area with access to a detailed computerized account of Van Gogh's life and times, while the third floor has a number of his sketches and a handful of less familiar paintings. The **third floor** also affords space to relevant temporary exhibitions illustrating Van Gogh's artistic influences, or his own influence on other artists, many of whom influenced his work – among them Gauguin and Millet.

To the rear of Rietveld's building, and connected by a ground floor-level escalator, is the ultra-modern curved annexe, completed in 1998. Financed by a Japanese insurance company – the same conglomerate that paid $35 million for one of Van Gogh's *Sunflowers* canvases in 1987 – this provides temporary exhibition space. Most of these exhibitions focus on one aspect or another of Van Gogh's art and draw heavily on the permanent collection, which means that the paintings displayed in the older building are regularly rotated.

VAN GOGH'S THE YELLOW HOUSE

THE MUSEUM QUARTER AND THE VONDELPARK

THE STEDELIJK MUSEUM

Paulus Potterstraat 13 ☎ 020/ 573 2911. Ⓦ www.stedelijk.nl Tues & Wed 11am–5pm, Thurs 11am–10pm, Fri–Sun 11am–6pm Closed Mon. €15. MAP P.96, POCKET MAP B7

The **Stedelijk Museum** has long been Amsterdam's number one venue for modern and contemporary art and finally, after moving hither and thither, it has returned to its original home, a big, old building that has been completely refurbished and updated. The museum focuses on cutting-edge, **temporary exhibitions** of modern art, from photography and video through to sculpture and collage, and these are supplemented by a regularly rotated selection from the museum's large and wide-ranging **permanent collection**. Amongst many highlights, the latter includes a particularly large sample of the work of **Piet Mondriaan** (1872–1944), from his early, muddy abstracts to the boldly coloured rectangular blocks for which he's most famous. The Stedelijk is also strong on **Kasimir Malevich** (1878–1935), whose dense attempts at Cubism lead to the

dynamism and bold, primary tones of his "Suprematist" paintings – slices, blocks and bolts of colour that shift around as if about to resolve themselves into some complex computer graphic. Other high spots include several **Marc Chagall** paintings and a number of pictures by American Abstract Expressionists Mark Rothko, Ellsworth Kelly and Barnett Newman, plus the odd work by Lichtenstein, Warhol, Robert Ryman, Kooning and Jean Dubuffet.

THE CONCERTGEBOUW

Concertgebouwplein 10 ☎ 020/573 0573; box office 020/671 8345, Ⓦ www.concertgebouw.nl English-language guided tours: Sun 12.15–1.15pm & Mon 5–6pm. €10. MAP P.96, POCKET MAP B7

The **Concertgebouw** (Concert Hall) is the home of the famed – and much recorded – Koninklijk (Royal) Concertgebouw Orchestra. When the German composer Brahms visited Amsterdam in the 1870s he was scathing about the locals' lack of culture and in particular their lack of an even halfway suitable venue for his music. In the face of

THE CONCERTGEBOUW

such ridicule, a consortium of Amsterdam businessmen got together to fund the construction of a brand-new concert hall and the result was the Concertgebouw, completed in 1888. Since then it has become renowned among musicians and concertgoers for its marvellous acoustics, and after a facelift and the replacement of its crumbling foundations in the early 1990s it is looking and sounding better than ever. The acoustics of the Grote Zaal (Large Hall) are unparalleled, and the smaller Kleine Zaal regularly hosts chamber concerts. Prices are very reasonable at €30–50, there are free Wednesday lunchtime concerts from September to May, and in July and August they put on a heavily subsidized series of summer concerts.

Tours last a little over an hour and take in the Grote Zaal, the Kleine Zaal, and the various backroom activities behind all this – control rooms, piano stores, dressing rooms and the like.

THE VONDELPARK

Several entrances off Van Baerlestraat ⓦ www.vondelpark.nl. Daily dawn to dusk. Free. MAP P.96, POCKET MAP A7

Amsterdam is short of green spaces, which makes the leafy expanses of the **Vondelpark**, a short stretch from Museumplein and the Concertgebouw, doubly welcome. This is easily the largest and most popular of the city's parks, its network of footpaths used by a healthy slice of the city's population. The park dates back to 1864, when a group of leading Amsterdammers clubbed together to transform the soggy marshland that lay beyond the Leidsepoort into a landscaped park. The park possesses over

THE VONDELPARK

100 species of tree, a wide variety of local and imported plants, and – among many incidental features – a bandstand, an excellent rose garden, and a network of ponds and narrow waterways that are home to many sorts of wildfowl. There are other animals too: cows, sheep, hundreds of squirrels, plus a large colony of bright-green (and very noisy) parakeets. During the summer the park regularly hosts free concerts and theatrical performances, mostly in its own specially designed open-air theatre.

The park is named after Amsterdam's foremost poet, **Joost van den Vondel** (1587–1679), who ran a hosiery business here in the city, in between writing and hobnobbing with the local elite. Vondel was a kind of Dutch Shakespeare and his *Gijsbrecht van Amstel*, in which he celebrates Dutch life during the Golden Age is one of the classics of Dutch literature. There's a large and somewhat grandiose statue of the man on a plinth near the main entrance to the park.

Shops

BROEKMANS & VAN POPPEL

Van Baerlestraat 92–94. Mon 10am–6pm,
Tues–Fri 9am–6pm, Sat 9am–5pm. MAP P.96,
POCKET MAP B7

Experts in classical music and
opera CDs and sheet music,
this shop has perhaps the best
selection in the city.

DAFFODIL

Jacob Obrechtstraat 41. Tues–Fri noon–6pm,
Sat noon–5pm. MAP P.96, POCKET MAP B8

Behind the Concertgebouw,
this fashionable and very
popular clothes shop features
secondhand designer labels,
mostly from the 1980s
onwards.

JACOB VAN WIJNGAARDEN

Overtoom 135. Mon 1–6pm, Tues–Fri
10am–6pm, Thurs until 9pm, Sat 10am–5pm.
MAP P.96, POCKET MAP A6

The city's best travel bookshop,
with knowledgeable staff and a
huge selection of books, maps,
inflatable and illuminated
globes and more.

ROBERT PREMSELA

Van Baerlestraat 78. Mon noon–6pm, Tues–
Fri 10am–6pm, Sat 10am–5.30pm, Sun
11am–5pm. MAP P.96, POCKET MAP B7

Great art and architecture book
specialist, with plenty of stuff
available in English.

WATERWINKEL

Roelof Hartstraat 10. Mon–Fri 10am–6pm,
Sat 10am–5pm. MAP P.96, POCKET MAP B8

The only thing on offer here
is water – over a hundred
different types of bottled
mineral water from all over
the world. If you're feeling
dehydrated –and flush – try a
bottle of the deluxe Bling H20
studded in Swarovski crystals;
at €49 a pop, it's the haute
couture of spring water.

Cafés and tearooms

KINDERKOOKKAFÉ

Vondelpark 6b (Overtoom 325) ☎ 020/625
3257. Daily 10am–5pm. MAP P.96, POCKET MAP A7

A café run by children aged
5–12, who cook, waiter and
wash dishes. Though this may
sound like a recipe for disaster,
the food – pizzas, sandwiches,
cakes – is simple and tasty and
it's all really good fun.

DE ROOS

PC Hooftstraat 183. Mon–Fri 8.30am–9pm,
Sat & Sun until 5.30pm. MAP P.96, POCKET MAP B7

The downstairs café at this New
Age centre on the edge of the
Vondelpark is one of the most
peaceful spots in the city,
selling a range of drinks and
organic snacks and meals.
There's also an upstairs
bookshop, and any number of
courses in yoga and meditation.

TOUSSAINT CAFÉ

Bosboom Toussaintstraat 26. Daily
9am–10pm. MAP P.96, POCKET MAP B5

This cosy, very friendly café not
far from the Vondelpark makes
a nice spot for lunch – excellent
sandwiches, toasties, *uitsmijters*

as well as a tapas-type menu, although service can be slow.

Restaurants

CAFÉ LOETJE

Johannes Vermeerstraat 52 ☎ 020/662 8173. Mon–Fri 11am–midnight, Sat 5.30–11.30pm; closed Sun. MAP P.96, POCKET MAP C8

Excellent steaks, fries and salads are the order of the day here at this *eetcafé*. The service can be patchy, but the food is great, and inexpensive. The pleasant outdoor terrace in the summer is a bonus.

GENT AAN DE SCHINKEL

Theophile de Bockstraat 1 ☎ 020/388 2851. Daily 11.30am–3.30pm & 5.30–10pm. MAP P.96, POCKET MAP A5

Situated just outside the top end of the Vondelpark, across the pedestrian bridge, this is a lovely corner restaurant on a busy canal, serving Belgian and fusion cuisine and a huge range of bottled Belgian beers to enjoy on their summer terrace.

DE ITALIAAN

Bosboom Toussaintstraat 29 ☎ 020/683 6854. Daily 5.30pm–11pm. MAP P.96, POCKET MAP B5

Dull name but the food is first-rate – Italian dishes, both à la carte and in a set menu – three courses for €25. The pizzas are cooked in a wood oven.

LE GARAGE

Ruysdaelstraat 54 ☎ 020/679 7176. Daily 6–11pm, Mon–Fri also noon–2.30pm. MAP P.96, POCKET MAP C8

This elegant restaurant, with an eclectic French and Italian menu, is popular with a media crowd, since it's run by a well-known Dutch TV cook. Call to reserve at least a week in advance and dress to impress. Three-course menus are €45.

ORIENT

Van Baerlestraat 21 ☎ 020/673 4958. Daily 5–10pm. MAP P.96, POCKET MAP B7

Excellently prepared Indonesian dishes, with a wide range to choose from; vegetarians are very well taken care of, and the service is generally good. Expect to pay around €20 for a *rijsttafel*.

POMPA

Willemsparkweg 6 ☎ 020/662 6206. Daily 11am–11pm.

A bright, modern daytime café serving a good line in tapas from €4, *Pompa* morphs into a cool Italian-accented restaurant by night offering everything from classic *pasta vongole* (€16.50) to steak with truffle pesto (€17.50).

Bars

WILDSCHUT

Roelof Hartplein 1. Mon–Fri 8.30am–12.30am, Sat & Sun 10am–12.30am. MAP P.96, POCKET MAP C8

Not far from the Concertgebouw, this bar is famous for its Art Deco trimmings, and its large and popular pavement patio. The nicest place to drink in the area, plus a decent bar menu.

Clubs

THE MANSION

Hobbemastraat 2 ☎ 020/616 6664, ⓦ www .the-mansion.nl. Club Fri & Sat 9pm–3am; bar Mon–Thurs 6.30pm–1am, Fri & Sat 6.30pm–3am; restaurant Mon–Thurs 7–11pm, Fri & Sat 7pm–midnight. MAP P.96, POCKET MAP C6

Brassy and over the top restaurant-cum-club with ostrich leather and gold leaf on the walls. Dress to impress and bring bags of money if you want to be a part of the jet set crowd.

The outer districts

Amsterdam is a small city, and the majority of its residential outer districts are easily reached from the city centre. The south holds most of interest, kicking off with the vibrant De Pijp quarter, home to the Heineken Experience and the 1930s architecture of the Nieuw Zuid (New South), which is also near the enjoyable woodland area of the Amsterdamse Bos. As for the other districts, you'll find a good deal less reason to make the effort, although the Tropenmuseum, a short walk from the Muiderpoort gate in Amsterdam East, is worth a special journey, and further south the Amsterdam ArenA, home to Ajax, is a must-see for football fans.

DE PIJP

MAP PP.104–105, POCKET MAP D7

Across Boerenwetering, the canal to the east of the Rijksmuseum and the Museumplein (see p.94), lies the busy heart of the Oud Zuid (Old South) – the district known as **De Pijp** ("The Pipe"), Amsterdam's first real suburb. New development beyond the Singelgracht began around 1870, but after laying down the street plans, the city council left the actual house-building to private developers. They made the most of the arrangement and constructed long rows of cheaply built and largely featureless five- and six-storey buildings, and it is these that still dominate the area today. The district's name comes from the characteristically narrow terraced streets running between long, sombre canyons of brick tenements: the apartments here were said to resemble pipe-drawers, since each had a tiny street frontage but extended deep into the building. De Pijp remains one of the city's more closely knit communities, and is home to a large proportion of new arrivals – Surinamese, Moroccan, Turkish and Asian.

Trams #16 and #24, beginning at Centraal Station, travel along the northern part of De Pijp's main drag, Ferdinand Bolstraat, as far as Albert Cuypstraat.

THE WETERING CIRCUIT

MAP PP.104–105, POCKET MAP D7

At the southern end of Vijzelgracht, on the city-centre side of the Singelgracht, is the **Wetering circuit** roundabout, which has two low-key memorials to World War II. On

THE HEINEKEN EXPERIENCE

ALBERT CUYPSTRAAT MARKET

the southwestern corner of the roundabout, by the canal, is a sculpture of a wounded man holding a bugle; it was here, on March 12, 1945, that thirty people were shot by the Germans in reprisal for acts of sabotage by the Dutch Resistance – given that the war was all but over, it's hard to imagine a crueller or more futile action. Across the main street, the second memorial in the form of a brick wall commemorates H.M. van Randwijk, a Resistance leader.

THE HEINEKEN EXPERIENCE

Stadhouderskade 78. Tram #16, #24 from Centraal station ☎ 020/523 9222, ⓦ www .heinekenexperience.com. Sept–May daily 11am–7.30pm, June–Aug daily 10.30am–9pm. €17, €15 if booked online. MAP PP.104–105, POCKET MAP D7

On the northern edge of De Pijp, just beyond the Wetering Circuit, the former **Heineken brewery**, a whopping modern building beside the Singelgracht canal, now holds the **Heineken Experience**. The brewery was Heineken's headquarters from 1864 to 1988, when the company was restructured and brewing was moved to a location out of

town. Since then, Heineken has developed the site as a tourist attraction with lots of gimmicky but fun attractions such as virtual reality tours and displays on the history of Heineken, from advertising campaigns to beer-making. The old brewing facilities with their vast copper vats are included on the tour, but for many the main draw is the free beer you get to quaff at the end in the bar.

ALBERT CUYPSTRAAT MARKET

MAP PP.104–105, POCKET MAP D8–E7

Ferdinand Bolstraat, running north–south, is De Pijp's main street, but the long east–west thoroughfare of Albert Cuypstraat is its heart. The general **market** here (daily except Sun 10am–5pm) – which stretches for over 1km between Ferdinand Bolstraat and Van Woustraat – is the largest in the city, with a huge array of stalls selling everything from raw-herring sandwiches to saucepans. Check out the ethnic shops that flank the market on each side, and the good-value Indian and Surinamese restaurants down the side streets.

THE SARPHATIPARK

Tram #3 & 25. MAP PP.104–105, POCKET MAP E8

Leafy **Sarphatipark** provides a welcome splash of greenery among the surrounding brick and concrete. The park, complete with footpaths and a sinewy lake, was laid out before the construction of De Pijp got underway, and was initially intended as a place for the bourgeoisie to take a picnic.

THE NIEUW ZUID

MAP PP.104–105, POCKET MAP B9

Southwest of De Pijp, the **Nieuw Zuid** (New South) was the first properly planned extension to the city since the concentric canals of the seventeenth century. The Dutch architect Hendrik Petrus Berlage was responsible for the overall plan, but much of the implementation passed to a pair of prominent architects of the Amsterdam School, Michael de Klerk and Piet Kramer, and it's the playful vision of these two – turrets and bulging windows, sloping roofs and frilly balustrades – that you see in some of the buildings of the Nieuw Zuid today. These architectural peccadilloes have helped make the Nieuw Zuid one of Amsterdam's most sought-after addresses. The best example of the area's style is the housing estate located just north of the Amstel canal, **De Dageraad** (see opposite). Apollolaan and, a little way to the east, Churchilllaan, are especially favoured and home to some of the city's most attractive properties. Locals pop to the shops on Beethovenstraat, the main drag running south right through the district, and stroll

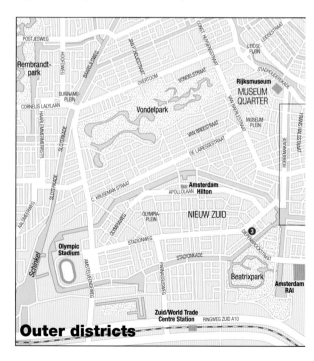

Outer districts

through the languid greenery of the Beatrixpark, or, slightly further out, the Amsterdamse Bos, but there's not much to attract the visitor who isn't a student of modern architecture.

THE AMSTERDAM HILTON

Apollolaan 138. MAP PP.104–105, POCKET MAP A9

One historic footnote that might entice you this far south is the **Amsterdam Hilton**, where John Lennon and Yoko Ono staged their famous week-long "Bed-In" for peace in 1969. More recently the *Hilton* was the centre of Dutch media attention when Herman Brood – a Dutch singer, painter and professional junkie – committed suicide by jumping from the roof.

DE DAGERAAD

Tram #4 runs along Van Woustraat; get off at Jozef Israelskade and it's a 5min walk to De Dageraad. MAP PP.104–105, POCKET MAP E9

Built between 1919 and 1922, the **De Dageraad** housing project was – indeed, is – public housing inspired by socialist utopianism, a grand vision built to elevate the working class, hence its name, "The Dawn". The handsome brick and stone work of the Berlage Lyceum marks the start of De Dageraad, with 350 workers' houses stretching beyond to either side of Pieter Lodewijk Takstraat and Burgemeester Tellegenstraat. The architects used a reinforced concrete frame as an underlay to each house, thus permitting folds, tucks and curves in the brick exteriors. Strong, angular doors, sloping roofs and turrets punctuate the facades, and you'll find a corner tower at the end of every block – it's stunning.

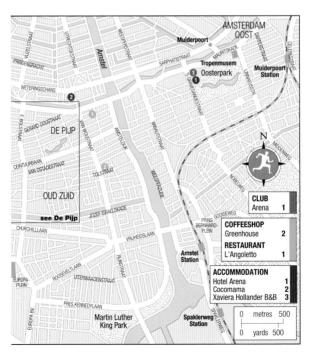

THE AMSTERDAMSE BOS

Main entrance near the visitor centre at the junction of Amstelveenseweg and Van Nijenrodeweg, 3km south of the west end of the Vondelpark (see p.98). Trams #16 & #24 from Centraal Station and the Heineken Experience (see p.103); it's about 350m from the nearest tram stop to the east end of Bosbaan and the visitor centre. ⓦwww.amsterdamsebos.nl. MAP PP.104–105, POCKET MAP B9

With ten square kilometres of wooded parkland, the **Amsterdamse Bos** (Amsterdam Forest), to the southwest of the Nieuw Zuid, is the city's largest open space. Planted during the 1930s, the park was a large-scale attempt to provide gainful work for the city's unemployed. Originally a bleak area of flat and marshy fields, it combines a rural feel with that of a well-tended city park – and thus the "forest" tag is something of a misnomer.

In the north of the Bos, the **Bosbaan** is a kilometre-long dead-straight canal, popular for boating and swimming, and there are children's playgrounds and spaces for various sports, including ice skating. There's also a goat farm at Nieuwe Meerlaan 4 (Wed–Mon 10am–5pm; ⓣ020/645 5034) and a nature reserve to the south with bison and sheep. Canoes and bikes can be rented west of the Bosbaan at **Kanoverhuur Amsterdamse Bos** (April–Sept daily 10.30am–7pm; ⓣ020/645 7831), Speelweide 5, on the Grote Vijver or "Big Pond" or you can simply walk or jog your way around a choice of six clearly marked trails. The **Bezoekerscentrum** (visitor centre; daily noon–5pm; free; ⓣ020/545 6100), at the main entrance to the Bos at

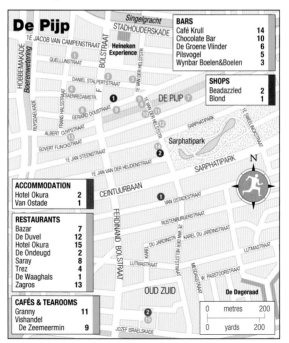

De Pijp

BARS
Café Krull	14
Chocolate Bar	10
De Groene Vlinder	6
Pilsvogel	5
Wynbar Boelen&Boelen	3

SHOPS
Beadazzled	2
Blond	1

ACCOMMODATION
Hotel Okura	2
Van Ostade	1

RESTAURANTS
Bazar	7
De Duvel	12
Hotel Okura	15
De Ondeugd	2
Saray	8
Trez	4
De Waaghals	1
Zagros	13

CAFÉS & TEAROOMS
Granny	11
Vishandel De Zeemeermin	9

Bosbaanweg 5, provides maps and information. There's also a pancake house, *Boerderij Meerzicht*, at the east of the Bosbaan at Koenenkade 56 (late Feb to Oct Tues–Sun 10am–7pm; Nov to mid-Feb Fri–Sun 10am–6pm; ☏020/679 2744) and bike rental close by (April–Oct daily 10am–6pm; ☏020/644 5473) – cycling being the best way of getting around.

COBRA MUSEUM

Sandbergplein 1, Amstelveen. Bus #170, #171 and #172, stop "Busstation Amstelveen" in front of the museum. ☏020/547 5050, ⓦ www.cobra-museum.nl. Tues–Sun 11am–5pm. €9.50. MAP PP.104–105, POCKET MAP B9

The **CoBrA Museum of Modern Art**, located well to the south of the Amsterdamse Bos entrance, close to the Amstelveen bus station, is soothingly white. Its glass walls give a view of the canal behind, displaying the works of the artists of the CoBrA movement, which was founded in 1948. The movement grew out of artistic developments in the cities of Copenhagen, Brussels

and Amsterdam – hence the name (a curled snake later became the symbol of the movement). CoBrA's first exhibition, held at Amsterdam's Stedelijk Museum, showcased the big, colourful canvases, with bold lines and confident forms, for which the movement became famous. The work displayed a spontaneity and inclusivity that was unusual for the art world of the time and it stirred a veritable hornet's next of artistic controversy. You'll only find a scattering of the paintings in the gallery, but there's enough to get an idea of what CoBrA were about, not least in **Karel Appel**'s weird bird sculpture outside, and his brash, childlike paintings inside. Appel, along with **Constant Nieuwenhuys**, was one of the movement's leading lights. Upstairs, the museum hosts regular temporary exhibitions of works by contemporary artists. There's a good shop, too, with plenty of prints and books on CoBra, plus a bright café where you can gaze upon Appel's sculpture at length.

THE MUIDERPOORT

Plantage Middenlaan. MAP PP.104–105, POCKET
MAP H6

Amsterdam East begins with Amsterdam's old eastern gate, the **Muiderpoort**, a grand Neoclassical affair through which Napoleon staged a triumphal entry into the city in 1811. His imperial pleasure was tempered by his half-starved troops, who could barely be restrained from helping themselves in a city of (what was to them) amazing luxury.

THE TROPENMUSEUM

Linnaeusstraat 2. Tram #9 from Centraal station or #14 from Dam Square. ☎ 020/568 8200, ⊕ www.tropenmuseum.nl. Tues–Sun 10am–5pm, also Mon during school holidays. €10, children €6. MAP PP.104–105, POCKET MAP H6

Despite its general lack of appeal, the East district does have one obvious attraction – the **Tropenmuseum**, perched on the corner of another of the city's municipal green spaces, the Oosterpark. Part of the **Royal Tropical Institute**, this large ethnographic museum has room to focus on themes such as the world's cultural and historical influences, and impresses with its applied art.

The first floor is dedicated to **Dutch colonialism**, focusing on Indonesia and the Pacific. Among the artefacts, there are Javanese stone friezes, elaborate carved wooden boats from New Guinea and, perhaps strangest of all, ritual ancestor "Bis poles" cut from giant New Guinea mangroves. The collection is imaginatively presented and there are also creative and engaging displays devoted to such subjects as music-making and puppetry. In addition there are intriguing reconstructions, down to sounds and smells, of typical settings from different

countries, such as a Jamaican café or a Surinamese logger's hut.

While you're here, be sure to try the inexpensive **restaurant**, the *Ekeko*, which serves tropical snacks and lunches, including popular national dishes from featured countries.

AMSTERDAM ARENA

Arena Boulevard 1. Metro to Strandvliet or ArenA ☎ 020/311 1336, ⊕ www .amsterdamarena.nl. Tours: 4–5 a day April–Sept 11am–4pm except match days, €12. Museum: April–Sept Mon–Fri 9.30am–6pm, Sat & Sun 10am–5pm, Oct–March Mon–Sat & last Sun of Month 11am–4.30pm, closed match days. €3.50. MAP PP.104–105, POCKET MAP F9

It's well worth the fifteen-minute metro ride to visit the **Ajax Museum** and take a tour of the stadium at the same time. The museum pays homage to Johan Marco Cruyff and van Basten and displays paraphernalia from the club's European campaigns. The main draw, however, is an hour-long, behind-the-scenes tour.

Shops

BEADAZZLED

Sarphatipark 6. Mon 1–6pm, Tues–Fri
10.30am–6pm, Sat 10.30am–5pm.
MAP PP.104–105, POCKET MAP D8

Beads in all shapes and colours
as well as bags, cheerfully
decorated lamps and other
accessories, bound to make
most women greedy.

BLOND

Gerard Doustraat 69. Mon noon–6pm, Tues–
Fri 10am–6pm, Sat 10am–5pm. MAP PP.104–105,
POCKET MAP D7

Popular gift shop with
hand-painted and personalized
pottery, bed linen, towels and
note blocks, mainly in the
colour pink.

Coffeeshops

GREENHOUSE

Tolstraat 91. Tram #4. Daily 9am–1am, Fri &
Sat until 2am. MAP PP.104–105, POCKET MAP F8

Consistently sweeps the boards
at the annual Cannabis Cup,
with medals for its dope as
well as "Best Coffeeshop" –
these guys are extremely
knowledgeable in their

"grassy" field. Tolstraat is
down to the south, but worth
the trek: if you're only buying
once, buy here. Also a branch
nearer to the centre at O.Z.
Voorburgwal 191.

Cafés and tearooms

GRANNY

1e van der Helststraat 45. Tues–Sat
9am–6pm. MAP PP.104–105, POCKET MAP D8

Just off the Albert Cuypstraat
market, adorned with
low-hanging beaded
lamp-shades and faded photos
of canal scenes, this place is
known for its terrific
appelgebak, had with whipped
cream for that full-on homely
experience.

VISHANDEL DE ZEEMEERMIN

Albert Cuypstraat 93. Mon–Sat 9am–5pm.
MAP PP.104–105, POCKET MAP D8

What better way to round off
your visit to the market than to
sample the delights of this
excellent – and typical – Dutch
fish stall. If you're not brave
enough for the raw herring
there are cooked offerings too,
such as calamari.

DE DUVEL

Restaurants

BAZAR

Albert Cuypstraat 182 ☎ 020/675 0544.
11am–midnight, Fri 11am–1am, Sat
9am–1am, Sun 9am–midnight; kitchen open
from 5pm. MAP PP.104–105, POCKET MAP D7

This cavernous converted
church is usually buzzing with
activity long after the market
traders have packed up. A lively
place to eat dinner; choose
from the Middle Eastern and
North African influenced menu
with tasty *mezze* and kebab.

DE DUVEL

1e van der Helststraat 59 ☎ 020/675 7517.
Daily 11am–4pm & 6–11pm, no lunch on Mon.
MAP PP.104–105, POCKET MAP D8

Immensely popular *eetcafé*, always crowded, so be sure to book ahead. Toasties and sandwiches at lunchtimes; mains such as steaks, *saté* and spaghetti at dinner for €16–20. Also a popular drinking spot.

HOTEL OKURA

Ferdinand Bolstraat 333 ☎ 020/678 7111.
Daily from 6.30pm. MAP PP.104–105,
POCKET MAP D9

This five-star hotel has two Michelin-starred restaurants – the sushi restaurant *Yamazato*, with over fifty specialities, and the *French Ciel Bleu* situated on the 23rd floor, offering amazing views of the city – plus the renowned grill-plate restaurant *Teppanyaki Sazanka*, which makes it one of the finest places to dine in the city. Reckon on at least €50 per person. Advance bookings essential.

L'ANGOLETTO

Hemonystraat 18 ☎ 020/676 4182. Daily
except Sat 6–11.30pm. MAP PP.104–105,
POCKET MAP E7

Just about everyone's favourite Italian, inexpensive and always packed, with long wooden tables and benches that create a very sociable atmosphere. Not everything they serve is shown on the menu, so keep an eye on the glass showcase in front of the kitchen for any specials. No bookings, so just turn up and hope for the best.

DE ONDEUGD

Ferdinand Bolstraat 13 ☎ 020/672 0651.
Mon–Sat 6–10pm. MAP PP.104–105,
POCKET MAP D7

A long time local favourite, presenting a French-oriented menu with the occasional Eastern twist. Prices are reasonable, with most mains €18–20, and the menu changes seasonally.

SARAY

Gerard Doustraat 33 ☎ 020/671 9216. Tues–
Sun 5–11pm. MAP PP.104–105, POCKET MAP D8

Excellent Turkish eatery down in the De Pijp neighbourhood. Its dark-wood, candle lit interior and living room ambience bestow an inviting backdrop for a leisurely dinner. It's cheap too, with main courses from €12.50 and mixed mezze €8 per person.

TREZ

Saenredamstraat 39 ☎ 020/676 2495. Tues–
Sun 6–10.30pm. MAP PP.104–105, POCKET MAP D7

Intimate little place, with good views of the chef cooking Mediterranean-inspired dishes in the open kitchen. Limited menu but very reasonably

TEPPANYAKI SAZANKA AT THE HOTEL OKURA

priced, with most main courses around €20 and set menus for around €25.

DE WAAGHALS

Frans Halsstraat 29 ☎ 020/679 9609. Tues–Sun 5–9.30pm. MAP PP.104–105, POCKET MAP D7

Well-prepared organic dishes in this cooperative-run restaurant near the Albert Cuyp. This place gets busy early so book ahead to be sure of a table. The menu changes twice a month, and though the food takes a while to prepare, the rewards are delicious and generously portioned. Mains around €18. No credit cards.

ZAGROS

Albert Cuypstraat 50 ☎ 020/670 0461. Tues–Sun 5–10.30pm. MAP PP.104–105, POCKET MAP C8

Popular no-frills Kurdish restaurant run by four brothers. Serves inexpensive traditional starters such as tahini and walnut salad from €3.50; mains including marinated lamb and chicken go for €13.

Bars

CAFÉ KRULL

Sarphatipark 2. Daily 10.30am–1am, Fri & Sat until 2am. MAP PP.104–105, POCKET MAP D8

On the corner of 1e van der Helststraat, a few metres from the Albert Cuyp, this is an atmospheric and lively place. Drinks and snacks all day long. Free wi-fi, good music and food too.

CHOCOLATE BAR

1e van der Helststraat 62a. Mon–Thurs 10am–1am, Fri & Sat 10am–3am, Sun 11am–1am. MAP PP.104–105, POCKET MAP D8

Cool, disco-inspired café-bar that's open for tasty food or cocktails any time of the day. Perch at the bar on leather stools or lounge in the cosy room out the back. It's a shame that service can be somewhat patchy.

DE GROENE VLINDER

Albert Cuypstraat 130. Daily 10am–1am, Fri & Sat until 3am. MAP PP.104–105, POCKET MAP D8

Great views on the bustling market from this split-level café with cheap daily specials and bulky salads.

PILSVOGEL

Gerard Douplein 14 ☎ 020/664 6483. Daily 10am–1am, Fri & Sat until 3am. MAP PP.104–105, POCKET MAP D7

Favourite drinking spot for style-conscious 30-somethings, enjoying the laidback atmosphere and decent tapas as well as the good selection of Spanish wines.

WYNBAR BOELEN&BOELEN

1e van der Helststraat 50. Tues–Thurs & Sun 6pm–midnight, Fri & Sat 6pm–1am. MAP PP.104–105, POCKET MAP D7

Tasteful wine bar close to Albert Cuypstraat market with a huge selection of wines. A heated terrace provides alfresco eating even in the cooler months, and the French-inspired menu offers seafood delights such as a half-dozen oysters for €14.

Clubs

ARENA

's-Gravensandestraat 51. Metro to Weesperplein, then an 8min walk ☎ 020/850 2400, ⓦ www.hotelarena.nl. Fri & Sat 10/11pm–4am. MAP PP.104–105, POCKET MAP H6

Hip club set in a restored chapel adjoining a hotel that used to be an orphanage and an asylum. Open Fridays and Saturdays, with occasional Salsa nights and special parties hosted on a Sunday. International DJs sometimes drop by – and that's when you can expect the entrance fee to jump from around €13 to €20.

Day-trips from Amsterdam

Amsterdammers may well tell you that there's nothing remotely worth seeing outside their own city, but the fact is you're spoilt for choice, with fast and efficient rail connections putting about a third of the country within easy reach on a day-trip. There are any number of places you can reach, including most of the towns of the Randstaad conurbation that stretches south and east of Amsterdam and encompasses the country's other big cities, The Hague, Utrecht and Rotterdam, but we've picked a few of the closest highlights. The easiest trip you could make is to Haarlem, just fifteen minutes away by train, a pleasant provincial town that is home to the outstanding Frans Hals Museum. There's also the showcase of the country's flower growers, the Keukenhof Gardens, worth visiting in spring and summer, while to the north of Amsterdam the most obvious targets are the old seaports bordering the freshwater IJsselmeer and Markermeer lakes, formerly – before the enclosing dykes were put in – the choppy and unpredictable saltwater Zuider Zee. No trains venture out along this coast, but it's an easy bus ride from Amsterdam, also taking in the beguiling one-time shipbuilding centre of Edam. Edam is, of course, famous for its cheese, but its open-air cheese market is not a patch on that of Alkmaar, an amiable small town forty minutes by train northwest from Amsterdam.

HAARLEM

HAARLEM

An easy fifteen-minute train journey (6 hourly) from Amsterdam's Centraal Station, **Haarlem** has a very different feel from its big-city neighbour. Once a flourishing cloth-making centre, the town avoided the worst excesses of industrialization and nowadays it's an easily absorbed place with an attractive centre studded with fine old buildings. The **Grote Kerk** (Mon–Sat 10am–4pm; €2.50), right in the centre of town on the Grote Markt, is well worth seeing, a soaring Gothic church with a magnificent eighteenth-century organ. But the real draw is the outstanding **Frans Hals Museum**, located in the Oudemannhuis or almshouse where the artist spent his last and, for some, his most brilliant years. Located at Groot Heiligland 62 (Tues–Sat 11am–5pm, Sun noon–5pm; €10; ☎023/511 57 75, ⓦwww .franshalsmuseum.nl), the museum is a five-minute stroll south from the Grote Markt – take pedestrianized Warmoesstraat and then Schagchelstraat and keep straight ahead.

The museum has a number of works by Haarlem painters other than Hals, with canvases by Jan van Scorel, Karel van Mander and Cornelis Cornelisz van Haarlem. Chief among the paintings by Hals is the set of "Civic Guard" portraits with which he made his name. Displayed together, these make a powerful impression, alongside the artist's later, darker works, the most notable of which are the twin Regents and Regentesses of the Oudemannenhuis itself.

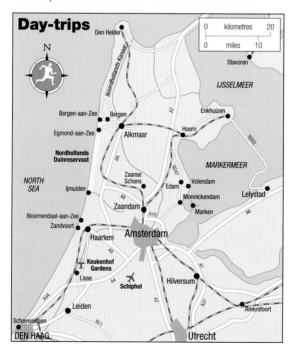

THE KEUKENHOF GARDENS

Stationsweg 166, Lisse ☎ 025/2465 555, ⓦ www.keukenhof.nl. Late March to late May daily 8am–7.30pm. €14.50.

The pancake-flat fields extending south from Haarlem towards Leiden are the heart of the **Dutch bulbfields**, whose bulbs and blooms support a billion-dollar industry and some ten-thousand growers, as well as attracting tourists in droves. The small town of **Lisse**, halfway between Leiden and Haarlem, is home to the **Keukenhof Gardens**, the largest flower gardens in the world. Its name literally meaning "kitchen garden", the site is the former estate of a fifteenth-century countess, who used to grow herbs and vegetables for her dining table. Some seven million flowers are on show for their full flowering period, complemented, in case of especially harsh winters, by 5000 square metres of glasshouses holding indoor displays. You could easily spend a whole day here, swooning among the sheer abundance of it all, but to get the best of it you need to come early, before the tour buses pack the place. There are several restaurants in the extensive grounds, and well-marked paths take you all the way through the gardens, which specialize in daffodils, hyacinths and tulips.

To get to the Keukenhof by public transport from Amsterdam, take the train to Leiden or Schiphol and take either bus #54 from Leiden station or #58 from Schipol Plaza. You can either pay on the bus or purchase a combination ticket (€21) online or at the tourist offices in Amsterdam, and at Schiphol airport, which includes bus transport from these locations and the entrance fee to the Keukenhof.

VOLENDAM

The former fishing village of **Volendam** is the largest of the Markermeer towns and was once something of an artists' retreat, visited by Renoir and Picasso in its day and always a favoured location for local painters. The Volendams Museum, on the edge of the town centre at Zeestraat 41 (mid-March–mid-Nov daily 10am–5pm; €3) has lots of local work on display, not least a series of mosaics made up of 11

million cigar bands, the work of a nutty local artist, and the comfy downstairs café of the *Hotel Spaander* on the waterfront is crammed full of seaside scenes and portraits contributed in lieu of rent over the years.

Volendam is reachable by bus #110 and #118 from outside Amsterdam Centraal Station; the journey takes half an hour.

MARKEN

Stuck out in the freshwater Markermeer, the tiny island of **Marken** was pretty much a closed community, supported by a small fishing industry, until its road connection to the mainland was completed in 1957. Nowadays, the fishing has all but disappeared, though the island – or rather its one and only village, Marken – retains a picturesque charm of immaculately maintained green wooden houses, clustered on top of mounds first raised to protect the islanders from the sea. There are two main parts to the village: waterfront Havenbuurt, which is dotted with souvenir shops, often staffed by locals in traditional costume; and the quieter Kerkbuurt, centred on the church, whose narrow lanes are lined with ancient dwellings and one-time eel-smoking houses.

You can take a ferry to Marken from Volendam (March–Oct daily 11am–5pm; every 30–45min; €8 return); the journey takes 25 minutes. The ferries leave you right in the harbour. Or you can get there direct from Centraal Station on bus #111 (every 30min; 35min). The bus drops passengers beside the car park on the edge of Marken village, from where it's a five-minute walk to the centre.

MARKEN HOUSE

EDAM

Considering the international fame of the red balls of cheese that carry its name, you might expect the village of **Edam**, just 12km or so up along the coast from Marken, to be jam-packed with tourists. In fact, Edam usually lacks the crowds of its island neighbour and remains a delightful, good-looking and prosperous little town of neat brick houses and slender canals. Nowadays, the one real crowd puller is Edam's **cheese market**, held every Wednesday morning from July to late August on the Kaasmarkt (10.30am–12.30pm), but the real pleasure is in aimlessly wandering its streets and canals, and maybe renting a bike to cycle down to the water. Bike rental is available at Ronald Schot, Grote Kerkstraat 7 (☎029/937 2155, ⓦ www.ronaldschot.nl); a day costs €6.50.

Bus #112 takes 40min to reach Edam from Centraal Station. The bus station is on the southwest edge of town, on Singelweg, a five-minute walk from the main square, Damplein.

ALKMAAR

Forty minutes north of Amsterdam by train, the small town of **Alkmaar** provides a pleasant glimpse of provincial Holland, with an old centre still surrounded by its moat, and a cluster of medieval and Renaissance-era buildings. It has some low-key things to see – the **Biermuseum De Boom** (Mon–Sat 1–4pm, April–Sept Fri 10am–6pm; €4), above the bar of the same name, has three floors devoted to the art of making beer, and opposite the town's main St Laurenskerk there's a local museum, the **Stedelijk Museum** (Tues–Sun 10am–5pm; €8), with paintings, maps and models of Alkmaar during its glory seventeenth-century years.

But the town is best known for its **cheese market** (mid-March to Sept Fri 10am–12.30pm), an ancient affair that these days ranks as one of the most extravagant tourist spectacles in the country. Cheese has been sold on the main square, Waagplein, since the 1300s, and although it's no longer a serious commercial concern, the market continues to draw the crowds. If you want a good view, get here early, as by opening time visitors are already thick on the ground. The ceremony starts with the buyers sniffing, crumbling, and finally tasting each cheese, followed by intensive bartering. Once a deal has been concluded, the cheeses – golden discs of Gouda mainly – are borne away on ornamental carriers for weighing. The porters, who bear the carriers, wear white trousers and shirt plus a hat whose coloured bands – green, blue, red or yellow – represent the four companies that comprise the cheese porters' guild. Payment for the cheeses, tradition has it, takes place in the cafés around the square.

From Alkmaar's train and bus station, it's a ten-minute walk to the centre of town: keep straight outside the station along Spoorstraat, take the first right down Snaarmanslaan and then left at busy Geesterweg, which leads over the old city moat to St Laurenskerk. From the church, it's another five minutes' walk east along Langestraat to the tourist office, housed in the Waag on Waagplein.

ALKMAAR CHEESES

Bars and restaurants

DAMHOTEL

Keizersgracht 1, Edam ☎ 0299/371 766. Daily noon–10pm.

The bar here is a cosy place for a drink, and it has a decent lunch menu of sandwiches, salads and pancakes for €6.75–10 and light mains for €16–18. Plus the hotel has the upmarket but excellent-value *Auberge* restaurant, which serves an ambitious menu of starters for €15 and rich and enticing mains for €25–30.

HET HOF VAN ALKMAAR

Hof van Sonoy 1, Alkmaar ☎ 072/512 1222. Mon–Wed 10am–9pm, Thurs 10am–9.30pm, Fri & Sat 10am–10pm, Sun 11am–9.30pm.

Pretty good for both lunch and dinner, a delightfully restored medieval nunnery that does inexpensive omelettes and sandwiches during the day and tasty Dutch cuisine in the evening, with mains for €15–20.

HOTEL SPAANDER

Haven 35, Volendam ☎ 0299/363 705. Daily noon–9.30pm.

This creaky old hotel right on the waterfront in Volendam is very much the hub of things in the town, with a nice bar for a drink or a coffee and a good brasserie serving lots of fishy specialities for lunch and dinner.

JACOBUS PIECK

Warmoesstraat 18, Haarlem ☎ 023/532 6144. Mon 11am–4pm, Tues–Sat 11am–4pm & 5.30–10pm.

Welcoming place that's a good bet for both lunch and dinner, with burgers and salads during the day and a Mediterranean-inspired menu in the evening with main courses for around €16.50. There's a secluded garden too.

JOPENKERK VESTESTRAAT

Haarlem ☎ 023/533 411. Daily 10am–1am, lunch noon–3pm, dinner 5.30–8pm.

This converted old church is a microbrewery bar and restaurant rolled into one, with long benches, comfy sofas and its own cloudy, unfiltered beer. The food is simple rather than splendid, but you should at least try one of the dozen or so Jopen brews at the bar.

LAND EN ZEEZICHT

Havenbuurt 6, Marken ☎ 0299/601 302. Daily 11am–8.30pm.

More of a lunch than dinner spot, but very cosy, overlooking the harbour and serving a mean smoked-eel sandwich.

STREMPELS

Klokhuisplein 9, Haarlem ☎ 023/512 3910. Daily 5.30–10pm.

Not a cheap option by any means, but the cooking is high quality and its four-course menu at €38.50 has to be one of Haarlem's (if not the country's) greatest dining bargains. They also have a brasserie that's open for lunch.

HOF VAN MARKEN

Buurt II 15, Marken ☎ 0299/601 300. Wed–Fri dinner only, Sat & Sun lunch and dinner.

This small hotel-restaurant, tucked away in Marken's back streets, has a cosy yet elegant dining room serving great food from a choice of three-, four- or five-course menus (for €36, €44 and €52 respectively). Choices include the likes of beef tartare with potato confit and horseradish, followed by steamed turbot, sea bass, or leg of lamb with aubergine couscous.

ACCOMMODATION

Hotels

Despite a slew of new hotels, from chic designer places through to chain high-rises, hotel accommodation in Amsterdam can still be difficult to find and is often a major expense, especially at peak times of the year – July and August, Easter and Christmas. Such is the city's popularity as a short-break destination that you'd be well advised to make an advance reservation at any time of the year. In spite of this, most hotels only charge the full quoted rates at the very busiest times, which means that you'll often pay less than the peak-season prices for double rooms quoted in this book; it's certainly always worth asking if there is any discount available, especially on week nights.

The Old Centre

GRAND HOTEL KRASNAPOLSKY > Dam 9 ☏ 020/554 9111, ⓦ www .nh-hotels.com. MAP PP.34–35, POCKET MAP B12. Located in a huge and striking mid-nineteenth-century building, this four-star hotel occupies virtually an entire side of Dam Square. Its rooms are nicely done, if unspectacular. Bargains are sometimes available. Breakfast not included. **€209**

HOTEL DES ARTS > Rokin 154–156 ☏ 020/620 1558, ⓦ www.hoteldesarts .nl. MAP PP.34–35, POCKET MAP B14. In a great location up near Muntplein, and very friendly. The more expensive rooms at the front are the ones to ask for in this moderately priced option. **€148**

HOTEL DE L'EUROPE > Nieuwe Doelenstraat 2–8 ☏ 020/531 1777, ⓦ www.leurope.nl. MAP PP.34–35, POCKET MAP B14. One of the city's top hotels, and retaining a wonderful fin-de-siècle charm, with large, well-furnished rooms, an attractive riverside terrace and a great central location. A canal view will cost you another €50 or so, but this is about as luxurious as the city gets. Breakfast not included. **€369**

LE COIN > Nieuwe Doelenstraat 5 ☏ 020/524 6800, ⓦ www.lecoin.nl. MAP PP.34–35, POCKET MAP B14. In a good location opposite the swanky *Hotel de l'Europe*, but a quarter of the price. All rooms have kitchenettes and are kitted out in contemporary fashion. **€139**

THE EXCHANGE > Damrak 50 ☏ 020/ 523 0080, ⓦ www.exchangeamsterdam. com. MAP PP.34–35, POCKET MAP B11. God knows, Damrak needs a decent hotel, and this new sister to the excellent *Lloyd Hotel* (see p.124) is a welcome and wacky newcomer. Each room has been "dressed" or designed by students of the Amsterdam Fashion Institute, so the decor can be eccentric to say the least (in one room you sleep in a giant tent) but it's certainly full of character. For the price, it's one of the best places to sleep in town. There's also a sleek downstairs coffeeshop, *Stock*. **€130**

MISC > Kloveniersburgwal 20 ☏ 020/330 6241, ⓦ www.hotelmisc .com. MAP PP.34–35, POCKET MAP C12. Excellent, very friendly budget hotel on the edge of the Red Light District, with six good-sized rooms each with a different theme. Breakfast included. **€145**

NES > Kloveniersburgwal 137–139 ☏ 020/624 4773, ⓦ www.hotelnes .nl. MAP PP.34–35, POCKET MAP C14. Pleasant and quiet hotel with helpful staff, and well positioned away from noise but close to shops and nightlife. It's also

Prices and tax

The least expensive hotels charge around €100 for a double room, a little less if you share a bathroom, but don't expect too much in the way of creature comforts at these sort of prices – you only really hit any sort of comfort zone at about €120-plus. Breakfast – bread, jam, eggs, ham and cheese – is often included in the price at the budget and moderately priced hotels, as is tax (five percent), but as ever the more expensive hotels slap both on top of quoted prices. One other thing to bear in mind: some of the cheaper hotels request full payment in advance or on arrival.

recently been given a bit of a facelift so rooms and public areas are much more consistent than before. **€129**

NH CITY CENTRE > Spuistraat 288 ☎ 020/420 4545, Ⓦ www.nh-hotels .com. MAP PP.34–35, POCKET MAP A13. A chain hotel, but an appealing one, in a sympathetically renovated 1920s Art Deco former textile factory, and well situated for the cafés and bars of the Spui and around. Some rooms have canal views, and all boast extremely comfy beds and good showers. Breakfast included. **€149**

SINT NICOLAAS > Spuistraat 1a ☎ 020/626 1384, Ⓦ www. hotelnicolaas.nl. MAP PP.34–35, POCKET MAP B11. Quirkier than many of the other three-star hotels in the area, the St Nicolaas's cosy downstairs bar-reception gives way to 27 comfortable refurbished rooms, all with baths. Conveniently located too, just five minutes' walk from Centraal Station. **€170**

PARK PLAZA VICTORIA > Damrak 1-5 ☎ 020/623 4255, Ⓦ www.parkplaza. com. MAP PP.34–35, POCKET MAP C11. This tall, elegant building opposite Centraal Station has been one of the city's best hotels for years. Its location couldn't be more convenient, and thanks to a much-needed refurbishment, each of its 164 rooms has a slick new look. Amenities include a fitness centre and pool. Breakfast not included. **€205**

WINSTON > Warmoesstraat 129 ☎ 020/623 1380, Ⓦ www.winston .nl. MAP PP.34–35, POCKET MAP C12. Part of the St Christopher's Inns chain, this self-consciously young and cool hotel has funky rooms decorated with crazy

art, and a busy ground-floor bar that has regular live music. It's a formula that works a treat; the *Winston* is often full – though this is probably also due to its low prices which include breakfast. Dorm beds available too, from around €35 a head during high season. Lift and full disabled access. Ten minutes' walk from Centraal Station. **€110**

Grachtengordel

AMBASSADE > Herengracht 341 ☎ 020/555 0222, Ⓦ www .ambassade-hotel.nl. MAP PP.54–55, POCKET MAP A13. Elegant canalside hotel made up of ten seventeenth-century houses with smartly furnished lounges, a well-stocked library and comfortable en-suite rooms. Free 24hr internet access. Breakfast is an extra €17.50, but well worth it. **€195**

AMSTERDAM AMERICAN > Leidsekade 97 ☎ 020/556 3000, Ⓦ www.edenamsterdamamericanhotel. com. MAP PP.54–55, POCKET MAP B6. Landmark Art Deco hotel just off Leidseplein that dates from 1900, though the bedrooms themselves are mostly kitted out in standard modern style. Large, double-glazed doubles; breakfast not included. **€140**

BACKSTAGE HOTEL > Leidsegracht 114 ☎ 020/624 4044, Ⓦ www .backstagehotel.nl. MAP PP.54–55, POCKET MAP B5. This hotel is aimed at musicians playing at the nearby *Melkweg* and *Paradiso*, and furnishings like theatre mirrors, spotlights and flight cases in the 22 rooms are designed to make them feel at home. Everyone can enjoy the free internet, 24hr bar and pool table. **€125**

Booking hotels

You can obviously book direct online or by phone, or you can compare prices and availability through the usual accommodation booking engines; one specific to Amsterdam is that of the Amsterdam Tourism Board – W www .amsterdamtourist.nl. Once you've arrived, the city's tourist offices (see p.135) will make on-the-spot hotel reservations on your behalf for a small fee, but during peak periods and weekends they get extremely busy with long and time-consuming queues. The good news is that the city's compactness means that you'll almost inevitably end up somewhere central.

CHIC & BASIC > Herengracht 13 T 020/522 2345, W www.chicandbasic .com. MAP PP.54–55, POCKET MAP B10. Dutch branch of this spunky Spanish concept, with 26 basic but cool rooms, some overlooking the canal. The changeable lighting allows you to adjust the colour of your room according to your mood – a cheapo gimmick, but an effective one. Breakfast not included. **€125**

CLEMENS > Raadhuisstraat 39 T 020/624 6089, W www .clemenshotel.nl. MAP PP.54–55, POCKET MAP C3. Well-run budget hotel in a good location close to the Anne Frank Huis, and one of the better options along this busy main road. Breakfast is extra. All rooms offer free internet, and you can rent laptops for just a few euros. Doubles with shower are more expensive. **€60**

DIKKER & THIJS FENICE > Prinsengracht 444 T 020/620 1212, W www.dtfh.nl. MAP PP.54–55, POCKET MAP C5. Small and stylish hotel not far from Leidseplein. Rooms vary in decor but all include a minibar, telephone and TV. Those on the top floor have good views of the city. **€175**

DYLAN > Keizersgracht 384 T 020 /530 2010, W www.dylanamsterdam. com. MAP PP.54–55, POCKET MAP C4. This stylish hotel is housed in a seventeenth-century building that centres on a beautiful courtyard and terrace. Its 41 sumptuous rooms range in style from opulent reds or greens to minimal white decor. The Michelin-starred restaurant offers French cuisine and the bar is open to non-guests. Luxury suites overlooking the Keizersgracht canal will set you back €1000. Breakfast is €28 extra. **€375**

ESTHEREA > Singel 303–309 T 020/624 5146, W www.estherea .nl. MAP PP.54–55, POCKET MAP A13. Comfortable four-star converted from a couple of sympathetically modernized canal houses. There's no hankering after minimalism here, with thick, plush carpets and beds that you literally sink into. Excludes breakfast. **€180**

HEGRA > Herengracht 269 T 020/623 7877, W www.hotelhegra.nl. MAP PP.54–55, POCKET MAP A13. This family-run hotel has a welcoming atmosphere and is pretty good value considering the location, on a handsome stretch of canal near the Spui. Recently refurbished rooms are small but comfortable. Breakfast included. **€135**

'T HOTEL > Leliegracht 18 T 020/422 2741, W www.thotel. nl. MAP PP.54–55, POCKET MAP A11. Appealing hotel located in an old high-gabled house along a quiet stretch of canal. The eight spacious rooms are decorated in bright, modern style with large beds and either bath or shower. No groups. Minimum three-night stay at the weekend; includes breakfast. **€170**

HOTEL 717 > Prinsengracht 717 T 020/427 0717, W www.717hotel.nl. MAP PP.54–55, POCKET MAP C5. Very exclusive canal house hotel with just eight suites, all individually designed. Great, large spaces, beautifully conceived, and perhaps the most luxurious small hotel in the city. **€500**

DE LEYDSCHE HOF > Leidsegracht 14 T 020/638 2327, W www.freewebs .com/leydschehof. MAP PP.54–55, POCKET MAP C5. Just seven rooms in this handsome canal house in a great location on the Leidsegracht between Herengracht and Keizersgracht. Simple but comfy, and very welcoming. **€120**

MARCEL'S CREATIVE EXCHANGE > Leidsestraat 87 ☎ 020/622 9834, Ⓦ www.marcelamsterdam.com. MAP PP.54–55, POCKET MAP C5. Popular B&B run by an English-speaking graphic designer and artist who attracts like-minded people to this stylishly restored house with four en-suite doubles available for two, three or four people sharing. Decor is chic and comfortable. Relaxing and peaceful amid the buzz of the city. You'll need to book well in advance in high season. Breakfast isn't included, but there are tea- and coffee-making facilities. **€120**

WEBER > Marnixstraat 397 ☎ 020/627 2327, Ⓦ www.hotelweber.nl. MAP PP.54–55, POCKET MAP B5. Seven spacious studio apartments decorated in a brisk, modern style above a popular bar, mainly attracting a youthful clientele. Small in-room breakfast provided. **€130**

PRINSENHOF > Prinsengracht 810 ☎ 020/623 1772, Ⓦ www .hotelprinsenhof.com. MAP PP.54–55, POCKET MAP E6. Tastefully decorated, this is one of the city's top budget options. Booking essential. Tram #4 from Centraal Station to Prinsengracht. Cheaper rooms without shower. **€89**

REMBRANDT SQUARE HOTEL > Rembrandtplein 24 ☎ 020/620 0652, Ⓦ www.rembrandtsquarehotel.com. MAP PP.54–55, POCKET MAP C14 Cheerful one-star hotel with an urban feel, located just off the busy Rembrandtplein. Rooms are all well equipped and tastefully decorated in various colourful shades. Tram #4 or #9 to Rembrandtplein. **€70**

SEVEN BRIDGES > Reguliersgracht 31 ☎ 020/623 1329, Ⓦ www .sevenbridgeshotel.nl. MAP PP.54–55, POCKET MAP E5. Very charming place – and excellent value for money. It takes its name from its canalside location, which affords a view of seven dinky little bridges. Beautifully decorated in an antique style, its spotless rooms

are regularly revamped. Small and popular, so reservations are pretty much essential. Breakfast is included in the price and served in your room. Trams #16, #24 or #25 from Centraal Station to Keizersgracht. **€120**

THE TIMES HOTEL > Herengracht 135 ☎ 020/330 6030, Ⓦ www .thetimeshotel.nl. MAP PP.54–55, POCKET MAP A11. Colourful designer hotel with a wink to the old Dutch masters – it's decked out with reproductions of paintings by Rembrandt, Vermeer et al. in every room. Good location, and free wi-fi. Excludes breakfast. **€159**

TOREN > Keizersgracht 164 ☎ 020/622 6033, Ⓦ www.hoteltoren .nl. MAP PP.54–55, POCKET MAP C3. Retro-chic boutique hotel, converted from two elegant canal houses. All rooms have been renovated, some have large jacuzzis and there's also an annexe. There's a breakfast room downstairs and they offer an adapted menu from nearby *Christophe* restaurant if you want to eat in the evening. **€180**

WIECHMANN > Prinsengracht 328–332 ☎ 020/626 3321, Ⓦ www .hotelwiechmann.nl. MAP PP.54–55, POCKET MAP C4. Family-run for over fifty years, this hotel occupies an attractively restored canal house close to the Anne Frank Huis, with dark wooden beams and restrained style throughout. Large, bright rooms are in perfect condition with TV and shower. **€140**

The Jordaan and the Western docklands

ACACIA > Lindengracht 251 ☎ 020/622 1460, Ⓦ www.hotelacacia .nl. MAP P.73, POCKET MAP B2. Small hotel situated in the heart of the Jordaan, right on a corner, so some of the rooms have wide views of the canal and its adjoining streets. Rooms, which sleep two to four people, are rather nondescript with small beds and a shower room. There are also self-catering studios (€100). Includes breakfast. **€95**

VAN ONNA > Bloemgracht 102 ☎020/626 5801, ⓦwww.hotelvanonna .nl. MAP P.73, POCKET MAP B3. A quiet, well-maintained place on a tranquil canal. The building dates back over three hundred years and still retains some of its original fixtures, though the rooms themselves are rather modest, with basic furniture and blankets on beds. No TV, no smoking and cash payment only. Booking advised. Includes breakfast. **€95**

The Old Jewish Quarter and the Eastern docklands

ADOLESCE > Nieuwe Keizersgracht 26 ☎020/626 3959, ⓦwww.adolesce .nl. MAP PP.82–83, POCKET MAP F5. Popular and welcoming no-frills hotel in an old canal house not far from Waterlooplein. There are ten neat and trim modern rooms and a large dining room. No breakfast. Triples are also available (€135). **€120**

LLOYD HOTEL > Oostelijke Handelskade 34 ☎020/561 3636, ⓦwww.lloydhotel.com. MAP PP.82–83, POCKET MAP H3. Situated in the up-and-coming Oosterdok district, this former workers' hostel has been renovated to become Amsterdam's coolest hotel. Rather pretentiously subtitled a "cultural embassy" (it has an arts centre and library), the rooms range from one-star affairs to five-star offerings. Some rooms are great, others not so – don't be afraid to ask to change. The location is better than you might think – just five minutes' by tram #26 from Centraal Station but at these prices you still might prefer to be in the centre. One-star **€100**, five-star, **€250**

The Museum Quarter and the Vondelpark

BILDERBERG HOTEL JAN LUYKEN > Jan Luykenstraat 58 ☎020/573 0730, ⓦwww.janluyken.nl. MAP P.96, POCKET MAP B6. Good-sized, nicely refurbished rooms mark out this decent stab at a mini four-star, full-service hotel. There's wi-fi in rooms, 24hr room service and a nice lounge and bar too. **€150**

COLLEGE > Roelof Hartstraat 1 ☎020/571 1511, ⓦwww .thecollegehotel.com. MAP P.96, POCKET MAP C8. Converted from an old schoolhouse, the College is one of the most elegant and original additions to Amsterdam's hotel scene. Original because it's largely run by students from the city's catering school; elegant because of the sheer class of the refurbishment. **€195**

JL 76 > Jan Luikenstraat 76 ☎ 020/515 0453, ⓦwww.vondelhotels. com. MAP P.96, POCKET MAP B7. Just five minutes' around the corner from its sister hotel the Vondel, this is the latest in a chic mini-chain, with the same contemporary vibe and high standards. Rooms are cool, sleek and simple, with iPod docking stations, coffee machines and DVD players – and, hey, you can even watch TV in the bath. There's free wi-fi throughout, and a pleasant lounge downstairs with an honesty bar and iPad for customer use. **€250**

NL HOTEL > Nassaukade 368 ☎020/689 0030, ⓦwww.nl-hotel.com. MAP P.96, POCKET MAP B5. Pick of the lot in the area, with thirteen designer rooms decorated with funky wallpaper and plenty of Buddhas and tulips. Some rooms have access to a private patio. Breakfast not included. **€125**

OWL HOTEL > Roemer Visscherstraat 1 ☎020/618 9484, ⓦwww.owl-hotel .nl. MAP P.96, POCKET MAP B6. The reasonably priced doubles are relatively blandly furnished, but its location is nice and quiet, with a downstairs lounge opening onto a lovely garden, and – run by the same family for nearly forty years – the staff are a welcoming bunch. **€130**

PIET HEIN > Vossiusstraat 53 ☎020/662 7205, ⓦwww.hotelpiethein .nl. MAP P.96, POCKET MAP B6. Five minutes' walk from Leidseplein, this sleek three-star has large rooms with views over the entrance to the Vondelpark and slightly more expensive rooms in the modern annexe overlooking its peaceful back garden. There's also a comfy bar that's open till 1am. Lift access. **€175**

POET HOTEL > Jan Luykenstraat 44 ☎020/662 0526, ⓦwww. **poethotelamsterdam.com**. MAP P.96, POCKET MAP B6. The 64 rooms at this hotel are fresh and functional, plus there's a nice bar on the ground floor. Wi-fi and bicycle rent available. Breakfast included. **€120**

ROEMER > Roemer Visscherstraat 10 ☎020/589 0800, ⓦwww.hotelroemer **.nl.** MAP P.96, POCKET MAP B6. Sister hotel of the excellent *Vondel* and just as slick and stylish, this boutique hotel has a very pleasant garden out the back. Decor is funky and fun, with colourful paintings on the walls, sleek bathrooms and comfortable beds. **€200**

SANDTON HOTEL DE FILOSOOF > Anna van den Vondelstraat 6 ☎020/683 3013, ⓦwww.sandton **.eu/nl/amsterdaml.** MAP P.96, POCKET MAP A6. A lovely small hotel, with each room decorated according a different philosophical theme. It's all beautifully kept, nothing is too much trouble, and the garden outside is a rare Amsterdam treat. A bit of the way but handy for the Vondelpark. Breakfast €15. **€140**

VONDEL > Vondelstraat 26 ☎020/612 0120, ⓦwww.hotelvondel.com. MAP P.96, POCKET MAP B6. Part of a small chain of design-conscious boutique hotels that is beginning to dominate this part of the city, this place is as cool as its cousins, with black paint and light natural wood characterizing the lovely rooms. There's a pleasant bar and breakfast room and modern art decorates the walls of the common areas. Doubles vary in size. **€160**

The outer districts

HOTEL ARENA > 's-Gravesandestraat 51 ☎020/850 2400, ⓦwww.hotelarena **.nl.** MAP PP.82–83, POCKET MAP H6. A little way east of the centre, in a renovated old convent on the edge of the Oosterpark, this place has been thoroughly revamped, transforming a popular hostel into a hip three-star hotel complete with split-level rooms and minimalist decor. Despite the odd pretentious flourish, it manages to retain a relaxed vibe attracting both businesspeople and travellers alike. Lively bar, intimate restaurant, and late-night club (Fri & Sat) located within the former chapel. **€129**

HOTEL OKURA > Ferdinand Bolstraat 333 ☎020/678 7111, ⓦwww.okura.nl. MAP PP.104–105, POCKET MAP D9. Don't be fooled by the concrete, purpose-built facade: this deluxe five-star hotel comes equipped with all the luxuries you would expect, such as a health club and sauna, and even a shopping arcade. Rooms have huge marble bathrooms, and, in the suites, mood lighting and control units for the curtains. Two of its four restaurants (see p.110) have Michelin stars. If you're feeling flush you could book "The Suite", set over two floors with a suspended glass staircase, private butler and cinema; a night here will set you back €12,500. **€220**

VAN OSTADE > Van Ostadestraat 123 ☎020/679 3452, ⓦwww.bicyclehotel.com. MAP PP.104–105, POCKET MAP D8. Friendly place down a quiet residential street, not far from Albert Cuyp market in De Pijp. It bills itself as the "bicycle hotel", renting bikes for €7.50 per day and giving advice on routes and suchlike. Garage parking available, though you'll need to book in advance. Basic but clean en-suite two-, three- and four-bed rooms, with cheaper rates for shared facilities. Tram #25 from Centraal Station to 1e van de Helststraat. Breakfast included. **€115**

XAVIERA HOLLANDER B&B > Stadionweg 17 ☎020/673 3934. ⓦwww .xavierhollander.com MAP P.96, POCKET MAP B9. A bit out of the way in the chi-chi Nieuw Zuid, but this B&B, run by former madam, Xaviera Hollander, is a real Amsterdam experience, with a couple of kitschy rooms kitted out with semi-clad photos of the owner and lots of well-thumbed sex manuals. Both rooms have shared facilities, but it's still very comfortable and welcoming. **€110**

Hostels

The least expensive central option is to take a dorm bed in a hostel – and there are plenty to choose from: Hostelling International places, unofficial private hostels, even Christian hostels. Most hostels will either provide (relatively) clean bed linen or charge a few euros for it – frankly your own sleeping bag might be a better option. Many hostels also lock guests out for a short period each day to clean the place, and some set a nightly curfew, though these are usually late enough not to cause too much of a problem. Note that many hostels don't accept reservations from June to August, and most charge more at weekends.

The Old Centre

BOB'S YOUTH HOSTEL > Nieuwezijds Voorburgwal 92 ☏ 020/623 0063, ⓦ www.bobsyouthhostel.nl. MAP PP.34–35, POCKET MAP B11. An old favourite with backpackers, *Bob's* is a lively place with small, basic dorm beds for €18 per person, including breakfast in the coffeeshop on the ground floor. They also let four apartments (€70 for two people, €80 for three). Just 10 minutes' walk from Amsterdam Centraal Station.

BULLDOG HOTEL > Oudezijds Voorburgwal 220 ☏ 020/620 3822, ⓦ www.bulldoghotel.com. MAP PP.34–35, POCKET MAP C12. Part of the *Bulldog* coffeeshop chain, with a bar and DVD lounge downstairs complete with leather couches and soft lighting. Dorm beds with TV and shower start at €27, including breakfast, and there are also double dorms available and rooms for €90, as well as fully equipped apartments from €150 – all with bathrooms and TVs. Trams #4, #9, #16 or #24 from Centraal Station to Dam Square, then a 3min walk.

FLYING PIG DOWNTOWN Nieuwendijk 100 > ☏ 020/420 6822, ⓦ www .flyingpig.nl. MAP PP.34–35, POCKET MAP C11. Clean, large and well run by ex-travellers familiar with the needs of backpackers. Free use of kitchen facilities, no curfew, there's a late-night coffeeshop next door and the hostel bar is open all night. Justifiably popular, and a very good deal, with mixed dorm beds from €25 depending on the size of the dorm. Just a 5min walk from Centraal Station.

STAY OKAY > Stadsdoelen Kloveniersburgwal 97 ☏ 020/624 6832, ⓦ www.stayokay.com/stadsdoelen. MAP PP.34–35, POCKET MAP C13. The closest to Centraal Station of the two official hostels, with clean, semi-private dorms at €24.50 for members, who get priority in high season; non-members pay €27. Price includes linen, breakfast and locker, plus use of communal kitchen. The bar overlooks the canal and serves good-value if basic food, and there's a 2am curfew (though the door opens for three 15min intervals between 2am and 7am). Metro Nieuwmarkt, or trams #4, #9, #16, #24 or #25 from Centraal Station to Muntplein. See also the city's other HI hostel, the *Stay Okay Vondelpark* (see below), which has a greater choice of rooms.

Grachtengordel

HANS BRINKER > Kerkstraat 136 ☏ 020/622 0687, ⓦ www.hans-brinker .com. MAP PP.54–55, POCKET MAP C5. Well-established and raucously popular Amsterdam hostel, with around 600 beds. Dorms are basic and clean and beds go for €25 and upwards, and en-suite singles, doubles and triples are also available for €40 a head. The facilities are good: free internet after 10pm, disco every night, and it's near to the buzz of Leidseplein too. A hostel to head for if you're out for a good time (and not too bothered about getting a solid night's sleep). Walk-in policy only. Trams #1, #2 or #5 from Centraal Station to Prinsengracht.

INTERNATIONAL BUDGET HOTEL
> Leidsegracht 76 ☎ 020/624 2784, Ⓦ www.internationalbudgethostel .com. MAP PP.54–55, POCKET MAP B5. An excellent budget option on a peaceful little canal in the heart of the city. Small, simple rooms sleeping up to four with shared facilities cost around €32 a head, breakfast is extra, and twin rooms €80. Young, friendly staff. Trams #1, #2 or #5 to Prinsengracht.

The Museum Quarter and the Vondelpark

FLYING PIG UPTOWN >
Vossiusstraat 46 ☎ 020/400 4187, Ⓦ www.flyingpig.nl. MAP P.96, POCKET MAP B6. The better of the two *Flying Pig* hostels (see opposite), facing the Vondelpark and close to the city's most important museums. Immaculate and well maintained by a staff of travellers, who understand their backpacking guests. Free use of kitchen facilities, no curfew and good tourist information. Fourteen-bed dorms start at €21.90 per person and there are a few two-person queensize bunks, as well as double rooms(€44.90). Great value. Trams #1, #2 or #5 from Centraal Station to Leidseplein, then walk.

Our picks

BUDGET *Seven Bridges* > p.123
CENTRAL *Estherea* > p.122
BOUTIQUE *Vondel* > p.125
ROMANCE *Toren* > p.123
CELEBS *Dylan* > p.122
LUXURY *717* > p.123
GRUNGY *Winston* > p.121

STAY OKAY VONDELPARK > Zandpad
5 ☎ 020/589 8996, Ⓦ www.stayokay .com/vondelpark. MAP P.96, POCKET MAP B6. The better of the city's two HI hostels, with a bar, restaurant, TV lounge, internet access and bike shed, plus various discount facilities for tours and museums. Dorm rates vary enormously from €27 to €41 (members pay €2.50 less), including use of all facilities, shower, sheets and breakfast. Secure lockers and no curfew. To be sure of a place in high season you'll need to book at least two months ahead. Trams #1, #2 or #5 from Centraal Station to Leidseplein, then walk.

The outer districts

COCOMAMA > Westeinde 18
☎ 020/627 2454, Ⓦ www.cocomama .nl. MAP PP.104–105, POCKET MAP E7. This relatively new hotel-hostel is excellently located, footsteps from the main museums and also from the De Pijp neighbourhood. Once a notorious old brothel, it has been painstakingly transformed into a light, welcoming space. The ground floor emphasizes the hostel vibe with its communal kitchen and sitting room and has a nice mix of small dorms while the four private en-suite doubles on the upper levels would not be out of place in a boutique hotel, each individually designed. **Dorm beds €36, private rooms €100.**

Arrival

Arriving in Amsterdam by train and plane could hardly be easier. Amsterdam's international **airport** is a quick and convenient train ride away from the city's **international train station**, which is itself just a ten-minute metro ride from the terminus for long-distance and international buses.

By air

Amsterdam's international airport, **Schiphol** (☎ 0900/0141, ⓦ www .schiphol.nl), is located about 15km southwest of the city centre. Trains run from there to Amsterdam Centraal Station every ten minutes during the day, every hour at night (midnight–6am); the journey takes 15–20 minutes and costs €3.80 each. Taxi fares from Schiphol to most parts of the city centre are €40–45. The Connexxion bus service (☎ 038/339 4741, ⓦ www .schipholhotelshuttle.nl) departs from the designated bus stop outside the Arrivals Hall every half an hour (on the half-hour) from 6am to 9pm at a cost of €16 one-way, €26 return. The route varies with the needs of the passengers it picks up at the airport, but buses take about thirty minutes to get from the airport to the city centre. Tickets are available from the Connexxion desk in the Arrivals Hall.

By train

Amsterdam's **Centraal Station** (CS) has regular connections with key cities in Germany, Belgium and France, as well as all the larger towns and cities of the Netherlands. Amsterdam also has several suburban train stations, but these are principally for commuters. For all rail enquiries contact **NS** (Netherlands Railways; international enquiries ☎ 0900/202 1163; domestic enquiries ☎ 0900/9292; ⓦ www.ns.nl or ⓦ www.9292.nl).

By bus

Eurolines (☎ 088/076 1700, ⓦ www .eurolines.nl) long-distance, international buses arrive at Amstel Station, about 3.5km to the southeast of Centraal Station. The metro journey to Centraal Station takes about ten minutes.

City transport

Almost all of Amsterdam's leading attractions are within easy walking distance of each other. The city has a first-rate public transport system, run by the **GVB**. Centraal Station is the hub of the system, with trams and buses departing from outside on Stationsplein, which is also the location of a metro station and a GVB public transport information office. There's a taxi rank on Stationsplein too.

Tickets

The **OV-Chipkaart** (ⓦ www .ov-chipkaart.nl) is an electronic payment card which covers the cost of travelling on all of the GVB transport system. There are two main sorts of card – rechargeable plastic cards and disposable paper cards set to a predetermined value and length of time. They are sold at the tourist office and on the city's trams and at the metro. You must scan the card when you get on and off the bus, tram, ferry or metro. A disposable *dagkaart* (day ticket), for unlimited travel, costs €7.50 for 24 hours, €12 for 48 hours and €16 for 72 hours. Note that the GVB tries hard to keep fare-dodging to a minimum, and wherever you're travelling and at whatever time of day, there's a chance you'll have your ticket checked. If you are caught without a valid ticket, you risk an on-the-spot fine of €35.

Trams, metro and buses

Trams crisscross the city: two of the most useful are #2 and #5, which link Centraal Station with Leidsestraat and the Rijksmuseum every ten minutes or so during the day. **Buses** are mainly useful for going to the outskirts, and the same applies to the **metro**, which has just two city centre stations, Nieuwmarkt and Waterlooplein. Trams, buses and the metro operate daily between 6am and midnight, supplemented by a limited number of nightbuses (*nachtbussen*). All tram and bus stops display a detailed map of the network. For further details on all services, head for the main GVB information office (Mon–Fri 7am–9pm, Sat & Sun 10am–6pm; ☎ 0900/8011, ☺ www.gvb.nl) on Stationsplein. Its free, English-language *Tourist Guide to Public Transport* is very helpful, and it provides free transport maps too.

The Canal Bus

One good way to get around Amsterdam's waterways is to take the Canal Bus (☎ 020/623 9886, ☺ www.canal.nl). This operates on three circular routes, coloured green, red and blue, which meet at various places: at the jetty opposite Centraal Station beside Prins Hendrikkade; on the Singelgracht (opposite the Rijksmuseum), near the Leidseplein; and by the Stadhuis on Waterlooplein. There are fourteen stops in all and together they give easy access to all the major sights. Boats leave from opposite Centraal Station every half an hour or so during low season between 10am and 5.30pm (longer in high season), and a 24hr ticket for all three

routes, allowing you to hop on and off as many times as you like, costs €22 per adult, €11 for children (4–11 years old). The ticket also entitles the bearer to minor discounts at several museums. Two-day passes cost €33.

The Museum Cruise

For something different try the Museum Line (☎ 020/530 5412, ☺ www.lovers.nl) cruise, a pleasant trip that takes in the Anne Frank Huis, Rijksmuseum and Leidseplein. It departs from opposite Centraal Station (9 daily between 10am-5pm; Sat to 5.30pm). Tickets cost €15, children (4–12 years old) €7.50.

Boat tours

There are several **boat tour** operators and they occupy the prime pitches – the jetties near Centraal Station on Stationsplein, beside the Damrak and on Prins Hendrikkade. **Prices** are fairly uniform with a one-hour tour costing around €12 per adult, €6 per child (4–12 years old), and around €30 (€17) for a two-hour cruise at night. The big companies also offer more **specialized boat trips** – dinner cruises from around €60, literary cruises, and most notably the Amsterdam Historical Cruise run by Lovers (☎ 020/530 5412, ☺ www.lovers.nl; €11.50–23). All these cruises are popular and long queues are common in the summer. One way of avoiding much of the crush is to walk down the Damrak from Centraal Station to the jetty at the near end of the Rokin, where the first-rate Reederij P. Kooij (who also have a jetty beside Centraal Station) offers all the basic cruises at competitive prices.

Canal Bikes

You can rent **Canal Bikes** (☎ 020/626 5574, ☺ www.canal.nl) – four-seater **pedaloes** – at four central locations: on the Singelgracht opposite the Rijks-

Tour operators

Mee in Mokum Keizersgracht 346 ☎ 020/625 1390, ⓦ meeinmokum.nl
Guided walking tours of the old centre and the Jordaan by long-time – and
often older – Amsterdam residents. Tours run daily except Monday; €7.50
per person. Advance reservations required.

Reederij P. Kooij on the Rokin, beside the Queen Wilhelmina statue
☎ 020/623 3810, ⓦ www.rederijkooij.nl. Provides a range of cruises by day
and by night, at prices that are often cheaper than the rest. Also has a (more
crowded) jetty opposite Centraal Station on Stationsplein.

Yellow Bike Tours Nieuwezijds Kolk 29, off Nieuwezijds Voorburgwal
☎ 020/620 6940, ⓦ www.yellowbike.nl. Three-hour guided cycling tours
around the city (2 daily) that cost €19.50 per person, including the bike.
Advance reservations required.

museum; the Prinsengracht outside the
Anne Frankhuis; on Keizersgracht at
Leidsestraat; and behind Leidseplein.
Rental prices per person per hour are
€7 (3–4 people) or €8 (1–2 people),
plus a refundable deposit of €20. They
can be picked up at one location and
left at any of the others; opening times
are April to October daily 10am to 6pm,
until 10pm in July and August.

Bicycles

The city has an excellent network
of designated bicycle lanes
(*fietspaden*). The needs of the cyclist
often take precedence over those of
the motorist and by law, if there's a
collision, it's always the driver's fault.

Bike rental is straightforward.
There are lots of **rental companies** (*fietsenverhuur*) but MacBike
(daily 9am–5.45pm; ☎ 020/624 8391,
ⓦ www.macbike.nl) is perhaps the
most convenient, with three rental
outlets in central Amsterdam: one
at the east end of Centraal Station,
a second beside Waterlooplein at

Mr Visserplein 2, and a third near
Leidseplein at Weteringschans 2.
They charge €7 for three hours, €9.50
per day, €19 for three days and €30
for a week for a standard bicycle;
21-speed cycles cost about half as
much again. All companies ask for
some type of security, usually in the
form of a cash deposit (some will
take credit card imprints) and/or
passport.

Taxis

The centre of Amsterdam is geared
up for trams and bicycles rather
than cars, so **taxis** are not as much
use as they are in many other cities.
They are, however, plentiful: taxi
ranks are all over the city centre
and they can also be hailed on
the street. **Fares** are metered and
reasonably high, but distances are
small: the trip from Centraal Station
to the Leidseplein, for example,
will cost around €12, €3 more to
Museumplein – and about fifteen
percent more late at night.

Directory A–Z

Addresses

Addresses are written as, for example, "Kerkstr.79 II", which means the second-floor apartment at Kerstraat 79. The ground floor is indicated by *hs* (huis, house) after the number; the basement is *sous* (souterrain). In some cases 1e, 2e, 3e and 4e are placed in front; these are abbreviations for *Eersete* (first), *Tweede* (second), *Derde* (third) and *Vierde* (fourth). Many side streets take the name of the street they run off, with the addition of the word *dwars*, meaning "'crossing'" – for instance, Palmdwarsstraat is a side street off Palmstraat. The main Grachtengordel canals begin their numbering at Brouwersgracht and increase as they progress anticlockwise. T/O (tegenover or "opposite") shows that the address is a boat.

Cinema

Most of Amsterdam's commercial **cinemas** are multiplexes showing general releases, but there's also a scattering of film houses showing revival and art films and occasional retrospectives. The **Kriterion** at Roeterstraat 170 (☎020/623 1708, ⓦ www.kriterion.nl) is a stylish cinema close to Weesperplein metro that shows arthouse and quality commercial films, while the beautiful Art Deco cinema **The Movies**, at Haarlemmerdijk 161 (☎020/638 6016, ⓦ www.themovies .nl), shows independent films.

Drugs

Drugs, both hard and soft, are **illegal** in the Netherlands, however the country has long tolerated the possession and consumption of small amounts of cannabis (under 5g) in designated premises (coffeeshops). In 2012 it was proposed that non-Dutch citizens should be banned from entering coffeeshops to prevent "drugs tourism". At the time of writing it was unclear whether the ban would be enforced in Amsterdam. Other soft drugs including magic mushrooms and "space cakes" are sold openly but are also illegal.

Electricity

The Dutch electricity supply runs at 220V AC.British equipment needs only a plug adaptor; American apparatus requires a transformer and an adaptor.

Embassies and consulates

Australia Carnegielaan 4, 2517 KH The Hague ☎070/310 8200; **Canada** Sophialaan 7 2514 JP The Hague ☎070/311 1600; **Ireland** Scheveningseweg 112, 2584 AE, 2514 BA The Hague ☎070/363 0993; **New Zealand** Eisenhowerlaan 77N, 2517 KK The Hague ☎070/346 9324; **South Africa** Wassenaarseweg 36, 2596 CJ The Hague ☎070/392 4501; **UK** Lange Voorhout 10, 2514 ED The Hague ☎070/427 0427; **USA** Lange Voorhout 102, 2514 EJ The Hague ☎070/310 9209.

Gay and lesbian Amsterdam

Amsterdam is one of the top gay destinations in Europe: attitudes are tolerant, bars are excellent and support groups and facilities are unequalled. The age of consent is 16. For help and advice contact the Gay & Lesbian Switchboard ☎020/623 6565, ⓦ www.switchboard.nl (Mon–Fri noon–10pm). Consider timing your visit to coincide with Amsterdam Pride (ⓦ www.amsterdamgaypride. nl) end July/beginning Aug or Leather Pride (ⓦ www.leatherpride.nl) in late October and early November.

Health

Your hotel or the VVV should be able to provide the address of an English-speaking doctor or dentist if you need

133

one. Otherwise call the emergency number ☎ 112. **Minor ailments** can be remedied at a drugstore (*drogist*). These sell non-prescription drugs as well as toiletries, tampons, condoms and the like. A pharmacy or *apotheek* (usually open Mon–Fri 9.30am–6pm, but often closed Mon mornings) also handles prescriptions; centrally located pharmacies includes Dam Apotheek (Damstraat 2 ☎ 020/624 4331) Lairesse Apotheek (De Lairesse-estraat 40 ☎ 020/662 1022) and Apotheek Koek, Schaeffer & Van Tijen (Vijzelgracht 19 ☎ 020/623 5949).

Internet

Most hotels provide internet access or wi-fi to guests either free, or at a minimal charge. A central internet café is *Internetcafe* at Martelaars-gracht 11 (daily 9am–1am, Fri & Sat until 3am; ⊕ www.internetcafe.nl), just 100m from Centraal Station.

Left luggage

Centraal Station has coin-operated luggage lockers (daily 7am–11pm) and a staffed left-luggage office (daily 7am–11pm).

Lost property

For items lost on the trams, buses or metro, contact GVB customer services (☎ 0900/8011, ⊕ www.gvb .nl). For property lost on a train, go to the Gevonden Voorwerpen office at the nearest station; Amsterdam's is at Centraal Station, near the left-luggage lockers.

Mail

TNT operates the Dutch postal service under the name TNT Post.

For the police, fire service and ambulance call ☎ 112.

Stamps are sold at supermarkets, shops and hotels.

Money

Debit cards are now the norm, and most shops and restaurants accept these and all major credit cards. You'll find ATMs throughout the city. Bureaux de change are also scattered around town – GWK has 24-hour branches at Centraal Station and Schiphol airport. The VVV tourist office also changes money. For **lost** and **stolen** credit cards and travellers' cheques the relevant numbers are: American Express ☎ 020/504 8000; Mastercard ☎ 0800 022 5821; Visa ☎ 0800 022 3110.

Opening hours

The Dutch weekend fades painlessly into the working week, with many smaller shops and businesses staying closed on Monday mornings til noon. Normal opening hours are, however, Monday to Friday 8.30am/9am to 5.30/6pm and Saturday 8.30/9am to 4/5pm. Many places also open late on Thursday or Friday evenings. Sunday opening is becoming increasingly common, especially within the city centre, where most shops are now open between noon and 5pm.

Most **restaurants** are open for dinner from about 6 or 7pm, and though many close as early as 9.30pm, a few stay open past 11pm. Bars, cafés and coffeeshops are either open all day from around 10am or don't open until about 5pm; all close at 1am during the week and 2am at weekends. Night-clubs generally open their doors from 11pm to 4am during the week, though a few open every night, and some stay open until 5am at the weekend. **Museums** are usually open from Monday to Friday from 10am to 5pm and from 11am to 5pm on weekends. Galleries tend to be open from Tuesday to Sunday from noon to 5pm.

Phones

The international phone code for the Netherlands is 31. Numbers prefixed ☎ 0800 are free; those prefixed ☎ 0900 are premium-rate – a (Dutch) message before you're connected tells you how much you will be paying for the call, and you can only call them from within the Netherlands. Phone booths are rapidly disappearing but there is a light scattering at major locations, like Centraal Station. **Phone cards** can be bought at outlets like tobacconists and VVV offices, and in several denominations, beginning at €5. The cheap-rate period for international calls is between 8pm and 8am during the week and all day at weekends. There is good coverage for **mobile phones/ cell phones** all over Amsterdam. Pre-paid SIM cards are available in telephone shops (on the Rokin and around Kalverstraat) and in some supermarkets. To speak to the operator (domestic and international), call ☎ 0800 0410; for directory enquiries, dial ☎ 0900 8008 (domestic), ☎ 0900 8418 (international). The Dutch phone directory is available (in Dutch) at ⊕ www.detelefoongids.nl.

Smoking

Smoking (tobacco) is banned in all public places as well as in all restaurants, cafés and bars and even coffeeshops (see also p.7).

Time

The Netherlands is one hour behind UK time and 6 hours behind EST in the USA.

Tipping

You are expected to leave a tip if you have enjoyed good service – up to around ten percent of the bill should suffice in most restaurants, while hotel porters and taxi drivers may expect a euro or two on top of the fare.

Tourist information

There are two tourist offices – **VVVs** (pronounced "fay-fay-fay") – one on platform 2 at Centraal Station (daily 9am–7pm), and a second larger one across from the main station entrance on Stationsplein (Mon–Fri 9am–5pm, Sat 10am–6pm & Sun 10am–5pm). The two offices share one website at ⊕ www.iamsterdam. com. They sell a range of maps and guide books as well as tickets and passes for public transport. They also take in-person bookings for canal cruises and other tours, sell theatre and concert tickets, and operate an accommodation reservation service.

Tourist passes include the **Iamsterdam Card** (⊕ iamsterdam.com) which provides free and unlimited use of the city's public transport network, a complimentary canal cruise and free admission to the bulk of the city's museums and attractions. It costs €40 for one day, €5- for two consecutive days and €60 for three consecutive days. It's not a bad deal, but you have to work fairly hard to make it worthwhile. It's available from any branch of the VVV.

An alternative if you're staying for more than a couple of days is the **Museumkaart** (⊕ museumkaart .nl), which gives free entry to almost every museum in the whole of the Netherlands for a year; it costs €39.95, or €19.95 for under-19s.

For information about what's on in the city, there's either the VVV or the **Amsterdam Uitburo**, the cultural office of the city council, housed in a corner of the Stadsschouwburg theatre on Leidseplein (Mon–Fri 10am–7pm, Sat 10am–6pm & Sun noon–6pm; ☎ 020/795 9950). Listings magazines include the AUB's own monthly *Uitkrant*, which is comprehensive and free but in Dutch, or the VVV's *Day by Day in Amsterdam*.

Festivals and events

STILLE OMGANG (SILENT PROCESSION)

Sun closest to March 15 Ⓦ www .stille-omgang.nl.

Procession by local Catholics commemorating the Miracle of Amsterdam, starting and finishing at Spui.

KONINGINNEDAG (QUEEN'S DAY)

April 30

The highlight of the festival calendar: in celebration of Queen Beatrix's birthday, the entire city centre is given over to one massive party.

HERDENKINGSDAG (REMEMBRANCE DAY)/

May 4

Wreath-laying ceremony and two-minute silence at the National Monument in Dam Square, commemorating the Dutch dead of World War II.

BEVRIJDINGSDAG (LIBERATION DAY)

May 5

The country celebrates the 1945 liberation from Nazi occupation with bands, speeches and impromptu markets around the city.

Public holidays

January 1 New Year's Day
Good Friday (although shops open)
Easter Sunday
Easter Monday
April 30 Queen's Day
May 5 Liberation Day
Ascension Day
Whit Sunday and Monday
December 25 and 26 Christmas

HOLLAND FESTIVAL

Throughout June Ⓦ www.hollandfestival.nl.

The largest music, dance and drama event in the Netherlands, showcasing productions at venues around the city.

VONDELPARK OPEN AIR THEATRE

June–Aug Thurs–Sun only Ⓦ www .openluchttheater.nl.

Free theatre, dance and music performances throughout the summer, presenting anything from jazz and classical concerts through to stand-up comedy. The future existence of the theatre was uncertain at the time of writing, as its city government subsidy was under debate.

JULIDANS

First half of July Ⓦ www.julidans.nl.

Twelve- day festival dedicated to contemporary dance. It is held in numerous locations around the Leidseplein, with the Stadsschouwburg as its throbbing heart.

AMSTERDAM PRIDE

End July or early Aug Ⓦ www .amsterdamgaypride.nl.

The city's gay community celebrates with street parties held along the Amstel, Warmoesstraat and Reguliersdwarsstraat.

GRACHTENFESTIVAL

Third week in Aug Ⓦ www.grachtenfestival.nl.

International musicians perform at over ninety classical music events at historical locations around the three main canals, as well as the River Ij. Includes the Prisengracht Concert, one of the world's most prestigious concerts.

UITMARKT

Last weekend in Aug Ⓦ www.uitmarkt.nl.
Every cultural organization in the city, from opera to theatre, advertises its forthcoming programme of events with free preview performances held around the Museumplein, Vondelpark and Leidseplein.

OPEN MONUMENT DAY

Second weekend in Sept Ⓦ www .openmonumentendag.nl.
For two days monuments throughout the Netherlands that are normally closed or have restricted opening times throw open their doors to the public for free.

THE JORDAAN FESTIVAL

Second or third weekend in Sept Ⓦ www .jordaanfestival.nl.
A three-day street festival in the Jordaan. There's a commercial fair on Palmgracht, talent contests on Elandsgracht, a few street parties and a culinary fair on the Sunday afternoon at the Noordermarkt.

AMSTERDAM DANCE FESTIVAL

Late Oct Ⓦ www.amsterdam-dance-event.nl.
A five-day dance music festival, hosting hundreds of national and international DJs taking over venues across the city. Tickets for all events have to be purchased separately and tend to sell out quickly.

MUSEUM NIGHT

Sat in early Nov Ⓦ www.n8.nl.
A great opportunity to explore Amsterdam's museums in the wee hours. Most museums are open until 2am, hosting DJ performances, workshops and concerts.

CANNABIS CUP

Late Nov Ⓦ www.hightimes.com.
Five-day harvest festival with seminars, tours and music events held at the Nachttheater Sugar Factory (see p.71) and the Melkweg (see p.71), which also hosts a competition to find the best cultivated seed. Judging is open to the general public.

PARADE OF SINT NICOLAAS

Second or third Sun in Nov
The traditional parade of *Sinterklaas* (Santa Claus) through the city on his white horse, starting from behind Centraal Station where he arrives by steam boat, before parading down the Damrak towards Rembrandtplein. It all finishes in Leidseplein on the balcony of the Stadsschouwburg.

PAKJESAVOND (PRESENT EVENING)

Dec 5
Though it tends to be a private affair, Pakjesavond, rather than Christmas Day, is when Dutch kids receive their Christmas presents.

NEW YEAR'S EVE

Dec 31
Fireworks and celebrations are everywhere, and most bars and clubs stay open until morning. This might just qualify as the wildest and most reckless street partying in Europe.

Chronology

1200s > Amsterdam begins to prosper.

1425 > Digging of the Singel, Amsterdam's first horseshoe-shaped canal.

1530s > Inspired by Martin Luther and subsequently Calvin, Protestantism takes root.

1555 > Fanatically Catholic Habsburg Philip II becomes king of Spain and ruler of the Low Countries, including Amsterdam. Philip prepares to bring his heretical subjects to heel.

1566 > The Protestants strike back, purging churches of their "papist" reliquaries and shrines.

1567 > Philip dispatches a huge army to the Low Countries to suppress his religious opponents; the pre-eminent Protestant leader is William the Silent, Prince William of Orange-Nassau.

1578 > Amsterdam deserts the Spanish cause and declares for William, switching from Catholicism to Calvinism at the same time.

1579 > The seven northern provinces of the Low Countries sign the Union of Utrecht, an alliance against Spain that is the first unification of the Netherlands; the signees call themselves the United Provinces. The Spanish Netherlands (now Belgium) remain under Habsburg control.

Sixteenth century > The Golden Age. Amsterdam becomes the emporium for the products of Europe as well as the East and West Indies. By the middle of the century Amsterdam's wealth is spectacular.

1613 > Enlargement of Amsterdam begins with the three great canals of the Grachtengordel.

1648 > Peace with Spain; Dutch independence is recognized.

1672 > William III of Orange becomes ruler of the United Provinces.

1770–1790 > Amsterdam is split into two opposing factions – the Orangists (supporters of the House of Orange) and the Patriots (who are pro-French).

1795 > The French army occupies the United Provinces. Many of the Dutch elite's privileges are removed.

1814 > After Napoleon's defeat at Waterloo, Frederick William of Orange-Nassau is crowned King William I of the United Kingdom of the Netherlands, incorporating both the United Provinces and the former Spanish Netherlands. The seat of government becomes Den Haag (The Hague).

1830 > The provinces of what had been the Spanish Netherlands revolt against Frederick William and establish the separate Kingdom of Belgium. Amsterdam stagnates.

1914–18 > The Netherlands remains neutral during World War I.

1940 > In World War II, the Germans overrun the Netherlands.

1941 > The Germans start rounding up and deporting the city's Jews in earnest.

1942 > Anne Frank plus family and friends hide away in the back annexe in the Prinsengracht.

1944 > Betrayal and capture of the Franks; Anne dies in Belsen concentration camp, but her father – Otto – survives the war and publishes his daughter's diary in 1947.

May 1945 > The Allies liberate Amsterdam, but many die of starvation during the hard winter of 1945-6.

1960s > Amsterdam changes from a conservative city into a hotbed of hippy action.

1976 > The Netherlands decriminalizes the possession of soft drugs, principally cannabis. The first dope-selling "coffeeshops" open.

Late 1970s > Amsterdam's squatter movement booms.

1984 > The squatting movement has a series of major show downs with the police. There are mass riots.

Late 1980s > The squatter movement fades away.

1990s > Several huge redevelopment schemes are planned, most notably among the old docklands bordering the River IJ.

2000 > The Dutch parliament repeals the laws prohibiting brothels.

2001 > The Netherlands becomes the first country in the world to recognize gay marriages.

2003 > Two of Amsterdam's flagship museums, the Rijksmuseum and Stedelijk begin ambitious renovation projects that fall victim to a series of delays.

2004 > Filmmaker Theo Van Gogh is shot dead in Amsterdam by Mohammed Bouyeri, a Moroccan by descent, who is enraged by Van Gogh's cinematic treatment of Islam. Across the country, race relations become tenser.

2007–10 > Rebuilding of the Oosterdok begins but the underground Noord-Zuidlijn metro line is ill-fated from the start. Costs balloon, the tunnels fill with water and the foundations of several old houses are undermined. The completion date is delayed to 2015.

2011–2013 > The government announces new anti-drug laws that will ban tourists from entering coffeeshops and buying and smoking cannabis. Cannabis with more than 15 percent THC is reclassified as a hard drug. In the south of the country the first wave of coffeeshops close in May 2012 amid protests of discrimination by shop owners. A nationwide ban proposed for January 2013 is strongly contested by Amsterdam officials.

DUTCH

It's unlikely that you'll need to speak anything other than English while you're in Amsterdam. The following Dutch words and phrases should be the most you'll need to get by, though menus are nearly always multilingual.

Words and phrases

BASICS AND GREETINGS

yes	ja
no	nee
please	alstublieft
(no) thank you	(nee) dank u or bedankt
hello	hallo or dag
good morning	goedemorgen
good afternoon	goedemiddag
good evening	goedenavond
goodbye	tot ziens
do you speak English?	spreekt u Engels?
I don't understand	Ik begrijp het niet
women/men	vrouwen/mannen
children	kinderen

NUMBERS

0	nul
1	een
2	twee
3	drie
4	vier
5	vijf
6	zes
7	zeven
8	acht
9	negen
10	tien
11	elf
12	twaalf
13	dertien
14	veertien
15	vijftien
16	zestien
17	zeventien
18	achttien
19	negentien
20	twintig
21	een en twintig
22	twee en twintig
30	dertig
40	veertig
50	vijftig
60	zestig
70	zeventig
80	tachtig
90	negentig
100	honderd
101	honderd een
1000	duizend

Food and drink

BASICS

boter	butter
boterham/broodje	sandwich/roll
brood	bread
dranken	drinks
eieren	eggs
erwtensoep/snert	pea soup with bacon or sausage
groenten	vegetables
honing	honey
hoofdgerechten	main courses
kaas	cheese
koud	cold
nagerechten	desserts
patates/frites	chips/French fries
sla/salade	salad
smeerkaas	cheese spread
stokbrood	French bread
suiker	sugar
uitsmijter	ham or cheese with eggs on bread
vis	fish
vlees	meat
voorgerechten	starters
vruchten	fruit
warm	hot
zout	salt

MEAT AND POULTRY

biefstuk (hollandse)	steak
biefstuk (duitse)	hamburger
eend	duck
fricandeau	roast pork

fricandel	frankfurter-like sausage
gehakt	minced meat
ham	ham
kalfsvlees	veal
kalkoen	turkey
karbonade	chop
kip	chicken
lamsvlees	lamb
lever	liver
spek	bacon
worst	sausages

FISH

garnalen	prawns
haring	herring
haringsalade	herring salad
kabeljauw	cod
makreel	mackerel
mosselen	mussels
oesters	oysters
paling	eel
schelvis	haddock
schol	plaice
tong	sole
zalm	salmon

VEGETABLES

aardappelen	potatoes
bloemkool	cauliflower
bonen	beans
champignons	mushrooms
erwten	peas
hutspot	mashed potatoes and carrots
knoflook	garlic
komkommer	cucumber
prei	leek
rijst	rice
sla	salad, lettuce
uien	onions
wortelen	carrots
zuurkool	sauerkraut

COOKING TERMS

belegd	filled or topped
doorbakken	well-done
gebakken	fried/baked
gebraden	roasted
gegrild	grilled
gekookt	boiled
gerookt	smoked
gestoofd	stewed
half doorbakken	medium-done
rood	rare

SWEETS AND DESSERTS

appelgebak	apple tart or cake
gebak	pastry
IJs	ice cream
koekjes	biscuits
oliebollen	doughnuts
pannekoeken	pancakes
poffertjes	small pancakes, fritters
(slag)room	(whipped) cream
speculaas	spice and honey-flavoured biscuit
stroopwafels	waffles
taai-taai	Dutch honey cake
vla	custard

DRINKS

bessenjenever	blackcurrant gin
droog	dry
frisdranken	soft drinks
jenever	Dutch gin
karnemelk	buttermilk
koffie	coffee
koffie verkeerd	coffee with warm milk
kopstoot	beer with a jenever chaser
melk	milk
pils	Dutch beer
proost!	cheers!
sinaasappelsap	orange juice
thee	tea
vruchtensap	fruit juice
wijn (wit/rood/rosé)	wine (white/red/rosé)
vieux	Dutch brandy
zoet	sweet

PUBLISHING INFORMATION

This second edition published April 2013 by **Rough Guides Ltd**

80 Strand, London WC2R 0RL

11, Community Centre, Panchsheel Park, New Delhi 110017, India

Distributed by the Penguin Group

Penguin Books Ltd, 80 Strand, London WC2R 0RL

Penguin Group (USA) 345 Hudson Street, NY 10014, USA

Penguin Group (Australia) 250 Camberwell Road, Camberwell, Victoria 3124, Australia

Penguin Group (NZ) 67 Apollo Drive, Mairangi Bay, Auckland 1310, New Zealand

Rough Guides is represented in Canada by

Tourmaline Editions Inc., 662 King Street West, Suite 304, Toronto, Ontario, M5V 1M7

Typeset in Minion and Din to an original design by Henry Iles and Dan May.

Printed and bound in China

© Martin Dunford, Phil Lee and Karoline Thomas 2013

Maps © Rough Guides

148pp includes index

A catalogue record for this book is available from the British Library

ISBN 978-1-40936-244-9

The publishers and authors have done their best to ensure the accuracy and currency of all the information in **Pocket Rough Guide Amsterdam**, however, they can accept no responsibility for any loss, injury, or inconvenience sustained by any traveller as a result of information or advice contained in the guide.

5 7 9 8 6 4

MIX
Paper from
responsible sources
FSC™ C018179
www.fsc.org

ROUGH GUIDES CREDITS

Text editors: Lucy Kane and Andy Turner

Layout: Anita Singh

Cartography: Katie Bennett

Picture editors: Mark Thomas and Rhiannon Furbear

Photography: Roger Norum, Natascha Sturny and Mark Thomas

Proofreader: Richard Lim

Production: Linda Dare

Cover design: Sarah Ross

THE AUTHORS

Martin Dunford is also the author of Rough Guides to Rome, Italy and The Netherlands, among others. One of the founding members of Rough Guides, he is now a freelance writer, editor and publishing consultant living in London and Norfolk with his wife Caroline and two daughters.

Phil Lee A one-time deckhand in the Danish merchant navy, Phil Lee has been writing for Rough Guides for well over twenty years. His other books in the series include The Netherlands, Norfolk & Suffolk, Mallorca & Menorca, Belgium & Luxembourg and Canada. He lives in Nottingham.

Karoline Thomas is a former Travel Editor for Rough Guides, who now lives in Melbourne with her young family. Karoline's other books include the *Rough Guide to Amsterdam*.

ACKNOWLEDGEMENTS

Phil Lee would like to thank his editor, Andy Turner, for steering us through the process of creating this new Pocket Guide to Amsterdam. Thanks also to my ever-helpful co-authors, Karoline Thomas and Martin Dunford.

HELP US UPDATE

We've gone to a lot of effort to ensure that the first edition of **Pocket Rough Guide Amsterdam** is accurate and up-to-date. However, things change – places get "discovered", opening hours are notoriously fickle, restaurants and rooms raise prices or lower standards. If you feel we've got it wrong or left something out, we'd like to know, and if you can remember the address, the price, the hours, the phone number, so much the better.

Please send your comments with the subject line "**Pocket Rough Guide Amsterdam Update**" to ⓔ mail@roughguides.com. We'll credit all contributions and send a copy of the next edition (or any other Rough Guide if you prefer) for the very best emails.

Find more travel information, connect with fellow travellers and book your trip on ⓦ www .roughguides.com

READERS' LETTERS

Thanks to all the readers who took the trouble to write and email in with their comments and suggestions. In the particular, thanks to: Annemarie Beers; J. G. Brekelmans; Johanneke Braam; Eveline Colijn; Florentine van Ede; Sjoerd van Eeden; Kim Gaarthuis; Lieke Heerschop; Lindy Heijmering; Eke van Heynegen; Dave Himelfield; Marten Hoeksma; Richard Jones; Klaas de Jong; Lotte Keess; Sabine Koch; Robert van Kuyk; Joost van der Kwaak; Steve Longo; Rosa Lopez; Mette Luiting; Jeffrey Maisels; Chantelle Parsons; Fieneke Peters; Jan Pieter; Frank de Ruijter; George Saba; Manon Schilder; Richard Shaffer; Marissa Verdonk; Keeley Warren.

PHOTO CREDITS

Index

Maps are marked in **bold**.